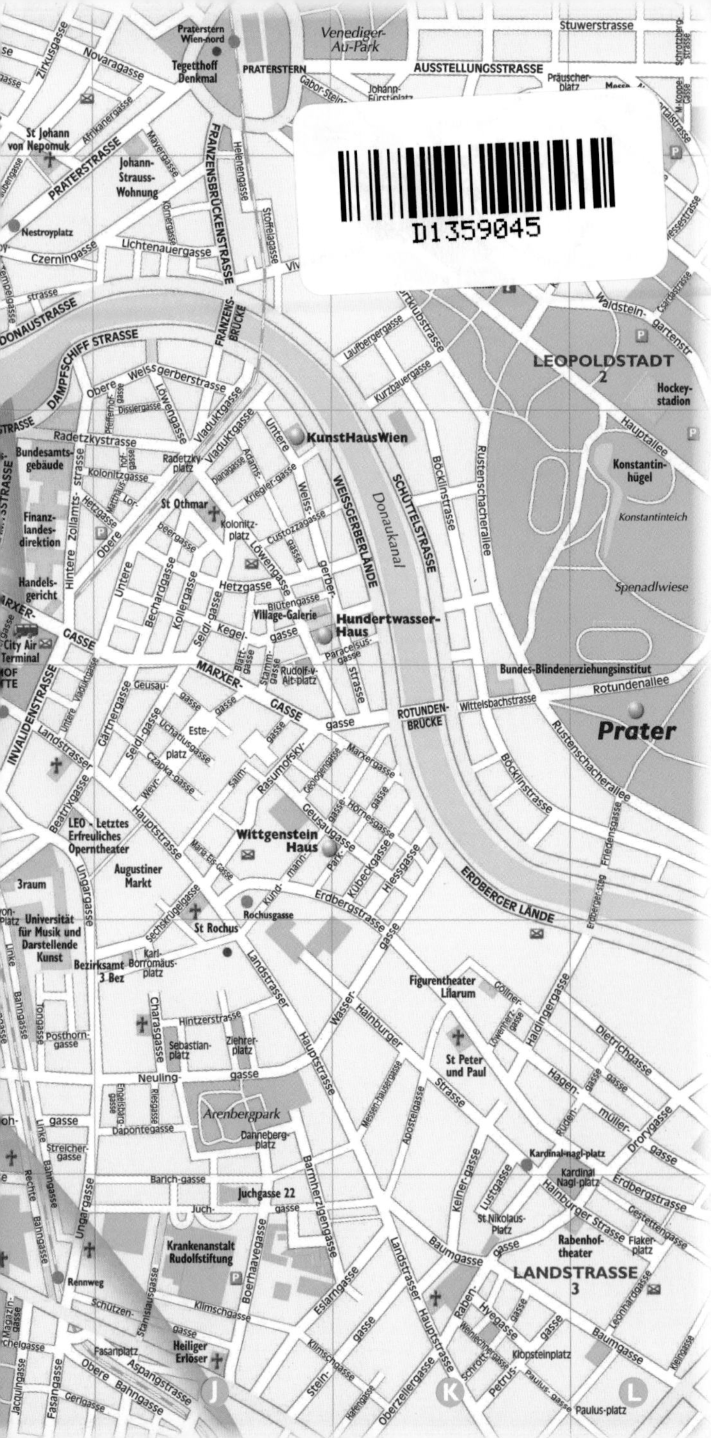
Praterstern Wien-nord
Tegetthoff Denkmal
PRATERSTERN
Venediger-Au-Park
AUSSTELLUNGSSTRASSE
Stuwerstrasse
Novaragasse
Zirkusgasse
St Johann von Nepomuk
Afrikanergasse
PRATERSTRASSE
Johann-Strauss-Wohnung
Mayergasse
FRANZENSBRÜCKENSTRASSE
Heinestrasse
Helenengasse
Stoffellagasse
Nestroyplatz
Lichtenauergasse
Czerningasse
DONAUSTRASSE
FRANZENS-BRÜCKE
DAMPFSCHIFF STRASSE
Obere Weissgerberstrasse
Löwengasse
Viaduktgasse
Radetzkystrasse
Radetzky-platz
Bundesamts-gebäude
Kolonitzgasse
Finanz-landes-direktion
Hintere Zollamts-strasse
Handels-gericht
St Othmar
Kolonitz-platz
Untere Weiss-gerber-strasse
KunstHausWien
Kriegler-gasse
Custozzagasse
WEISSGERBERLÄNDE
Donaukanal
SCHÜTTELSTRASSE
Böcklinstrasse
Rustenschacherallee
Laufbergergasse
Kurzbauergasse
LEOPOLDSTADT 2
Hockey-stadion
Hauptallee
Konstantin-hügel
Konstantinteich
Spenadlwiese
Waldstein-gartenstr
Hetzgasse
Bechardgasse
Kollergasse
Seidlgasse
Kegelgasse
Blütengasse
Village-Galerie
Hundertwasser-Haus
Paracelsus-gasse
Rudolf-v-Alt-platz
City Air Terminal
MARXERGASSE
INVALIDENSTRASSE
Geusaugasse
Gärtnergasse
Uchatiusgasse
Este-platz
Czapka-gasse
Weyrgasse
Rasumofsky-gasse
Salmgasse
Marxergasse
ROTUNDEN-BRÜCKE
Wittelsbachstrasse
Bundes-Blindenerziehungsinstitut
Rotundenallee
Prater
Landstrasser Hauptstrasse
Beatrixgasse
LEO - Letztes Erfreuliches Operntheater
Augustiner Markt
Wittgenstein Haus
Kundmanngasse
Kübeckgasse
Hiessgasse
Erdbergstrasse
ERDBERGER LÄNDE
Friedensgasse
3raum
Ungargasse
Universität für Musik und Darstellende Kunst
Rochusgasse
St Rochus
Sechskrügelgasse
Bezirksamt 3 Bez
Karl-Borromäus-platz
Linke Bahngasse
Tongasse
Posthorn-gasse
Charasgasse
Hintzerstrasse
Sebastian-platz
Ziehrer-platz
Figurentheater Lilarum
Wassergasse
Hainburger Strasse
Haidingergasse
Dietrichgasse
St Peter und Paul
Neulinggasse
Arenbergpark
Dapontegasse
Danneberg-platz
Streicher-gasse
Barichgasse
Juchgasse 22
Juchgasse
Barmherzigengasse
Apostelgasse
Kardinal-nagl-platz
Kardinal Nagl-platz
Kelsnergasse
Lustgasse
St Nikolaus-Platz
Rabenhof-theater
LANDSTRASSE 3
Erdbergstrasse
Baumgasse
Rechte Bahngasse
Krankenanstalt Rudolfstiftung
Rennweg
Schützengasse
Boerhaavegasse
Eslarngasse
Klimschgasse
Heiliger Erlöser
Fasanplatz
Aspangstrasse
Obere Bahngasse
Fasangasse
Jacquingasse
Obere Zellergasse
Steingasse
Hyegasse
Klopsteinplatz
Petrusgasse
Paulus-platz
Leonhardgasse
J
K
L
D1359045

Fodor's

25 Best

VIENNA

How to Use This Book

KEY TO SYMBOLS

- Map reference to the accompanying fold-out map
- Address
- Telephone number
- Opening/closing times
- Restaurant or café
- Nearest rail station
- Nearest Metro (subway) station
- Nearest bus route
- Nearest riverboat or ferry stop
- Facilities for visitors with disabilities
- Other practical information
- Further information
- Tourist information
- Admission charges: Expensive (over €10), Moderate (€5–€10) and Inexpensive (less than €5)

This guide is divided into four sections

• Essential Vienna: An introduction to the city and tips on making the most of your stay.

• Vienna by Area: We've broken the city into five areas, and recommended the best sights, shops, entertainment venues, nightlife and restaurants in each one. Suggested walks help you to explore on foot.

• Where to Stay: The best hotels, whether you're looking for luxury, budget or something in between.

• Need to Know: The info you need to make your trip run smoothly, including getting about by public transportation, weather tips, emergency phone numbers and useful websites.

Navigation In the Vienna by Area chapter, we've given each area its own color, which is also used on the locator maps throughout the book and the map on the inside front cover.

Maps The fold-out map accompanying this book is a comprehensive street plan of Vienna. The grid on this fold-out map is the same as the grid on the locator maps within the book. We've given grid references within the book for each sight and listing.

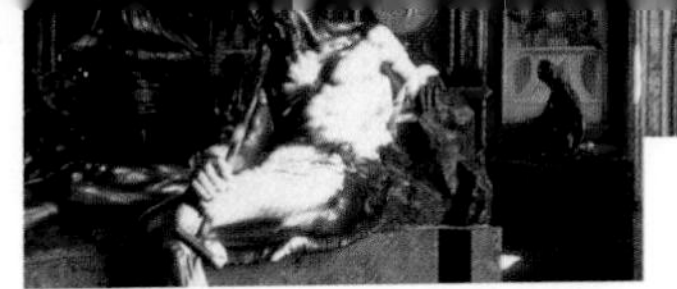

Contents

Introducing Vienna

Set in the heart of Central Europe, Vienna has always attracted visitors for its imperial treasures and outstanding cultural heritage. However, it is also gaining a reputation for being at the forefront of trends in fashion, cuisine and entertainment.

The Rathausplatz has become particularly lively. People gather here for ice-skating in winter, for the Social Democrats' 1 May parade and for the spectacular opening of the Vienna Arts Festival shortly afterward. There are open-air showings of music and opera films every evening in July and August, and from mid-November to Christmas Eve the glittering *Christkindlmarkt* is a major family attraction. It is also from here that the *Silvesterpfad* (New Year's Eve Walk) starts its meandering route toward Stephansplatz, where the Cathedral's great bell rings in the New Year while the crowds dance to the Blue Danube Waltz.

The Hofburg is another focal point of the city. In the Imperial Treasury you come face to face with the history of Central Europe, Habsburg power and the symbolic relics of Empire; if treasures are not your bag, you can see a musical performance at the Spanish Riding School; or, if you're prepared to rise early on a Sunday, go along to a sung Mass performed by the Vienna Boys' Choir in the Burgkapelle. But the "Burg" is not only a monument to the past; history is still being made here. Politicians, diplomats, officials and scientists from all over the world have been assembling in the Hofburg since Vienna became the third official seat of the United Nations.

The cosmopolitan metropolis of Vienna is not typical of Austria as a whole. It is rather an icon of the rich past of Central Europe; but at the same time it is ultramodern, a new economic hot spot, as its businesses take advantage of the fall of the Iron Curtain and seize new opportunities for investment.

FACTS AND FIGURES

- The population of Vienna is 1.73 million. The non-Austrian population of Vienna stands at more than 19 percent.
- Over 50,000 of the 185,000 pre-World War II Jewish-Viennese population died in the Holocaust.
- The metropolitan area has around 2.6 million inhabitants, meaning that one in five Austrians live in or near the capital city.

VIENNESE DIALECT

Viennese dialect is sophisticated and has a long tradition on stage and in cabaret, even in verse. Vivid, but impenetrable to outsiders, it is both a vibrant assertion of identity and a means whereby the Viennese can shelter their own private sphere in a city full of tourists and new arrivals.

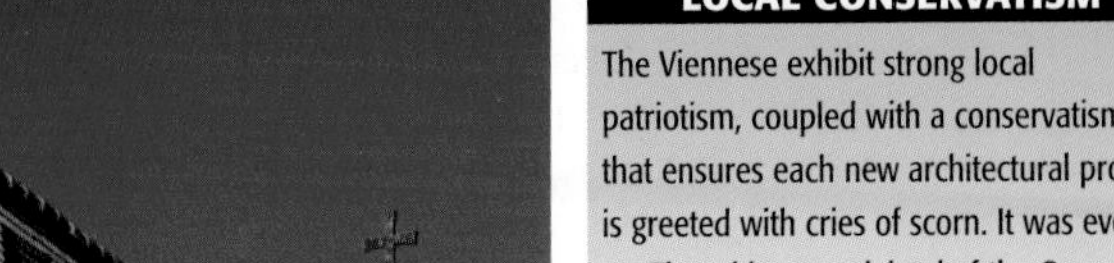

LOCAL CONSERVATISM

The Viennese exhibit strong local patriotism, coupled with a conservatism that ensures each new architectural project is greeted with cries of scorn. It was ever so: The critics complained of the Opera on its completion in 1869 that it looked like an "elephant lying down to digest its dinner."

MUST BE TIME FOR A MEAL

An astonishing 4,000 eateries cater to the Viennese need for meals at all times of the day. Extracurricular consumption includes at least one "coffee-pause" in the morning, and maybe a *Jause* (a hefty snack of bread, charcuterie and cheese) to stave off hunger pangs between serious eating. The locals cheerfully joke about "suicide by knife and fork," being no more perturbed by this prospect than their forefathers were by the scorn from medieval moralists (and the poet Schiller), who compared them to the Phaeacians, a gluttonous and pleasure-loving people in Homer's *Odyssey*.

A Short Stay in Vienna

DAY 1

Morning Start at the Opera (U-Bahn and tram stops). Just behind it is the famous **Hotel Sacher** (▷ 112) where you can enjoy a coffee and a slice of Sachertorte in the hotel's coffeehouse. Proceed to the nearby **Kapuzinergruft** (Capuchin Crypt, ▷ 29) on the Neuer Markt to view the tombs of the Habsburg emperors.

Mid-morning Adjacent to the Neuer Markt is Kärntner Strasse, from which you approach **Stephansdom** (St. Stephen's Cathedral, ▷ 31), the spiritual and topographical heart of the city. From the deeply sacred, move abruptly to the very secular: in a narrow backstreet behind the cathedral is the **Mozarthaus** (▷ 34) where the composer wrote his most satirical work, *The Marriage of Figaro*.

Lunch Enjoy a meal in the intimate garden of the **Haas & Haas** teahouse (▷ 39), accessed from the southwest corner of the cathedral square (Stephansplatz).

Afternoon From Stephansplatz walk north along the Graben, then turn left down the Kohlmarkt. Ahead of you is the vast complex of the **Hofburg** (▷ 26), the former Imperial Palace of the Habsburgs. Cross the Ringstrasse via the Heldentor to the **Kunsthistorisches Museum** (▷ 52) with its superb collection of pictures and applied art.

Dinner Across the River Wien a fine-dining experience awaits you at **Steirereck** (▷ 89), one of Vienna's finest restaurants.

Evening Close the day with a walk along the Ringstrasse to view the great Historicist architecture of the 19th century, beautifully illuminated at night.

DAY 2

Morning Start the day with breakfast in **Café Schwarzenberg** (▷ 62) opposite the **Hotel Imperial** (▷ 112) on the Ringstrasse. From there it is a short walk to the **Hochstrahlbrunnen** (▷ 85), a 19th-century fountain, and the huge Russian War Memorial behind it, both at the southern end of **Schwarzenbergplatz**. Then bear left and follow the Rennweg to the main entrance of **Schloss Belvedere** (▷ 82).

Mid-morning The highlight of the Lower Belvedere is the Golden Salon *(cabinet doré)* and Balthasar Permoser's statue (1721) of Prince Eugene of Savoy, whose palace this was. Climb the hill through the park to the Upper Belvedere with its splendid collection of paintings, including works by Klimt, Schiele and Kokoschka.

Lunch Try the traditional Viennese dish of *Tafelspitz* (boiled beef) at the nearby **Sperl** restaurant (▷ 89) and finish off with a *Powidltascherln*—the word may seem unpronounceable, but the sweet dumplings with plum compote are irresistible.

Afternoon For a complete change of theme and scene, take U1 (U-Bahn) from Südtirolerplatz-Hauptbahnhof to Praterstern. In the **Prater** (▷ 98) you can take a ride on the Ferris wheel or one of the many other attractions before going back to Schwedenplatz with U1. From here it is a short walk to the **Jewish Quarter** (▷ 28) and Judenplatz.

Dinner Indulge in some people-watching in the glassed terrace of one of Vienna's top Italian restaurants, **Fabios** (▷ 44).

Evening Take in an opera performance in the **Staatsoper** (▷ 35) or a concert in the gilded auditorium of the **Musikverein** (▷ 88).

Top 25

TOP 25

Akademie der Bildenden Künste ▷ **50** World-renowned gallery with five centuries of art.

Burgtheater ▷ **51** This theater has a staircase partly decorated by the young Klimt and his brother.

Coffeehouses ▷ **24** The soul of Vienna can be found in a coffee cup and topped by whipped cream.

Wien Museum ▷ **84** One of Europe's best city museums tells the history of the city from the Celts onward.

Stephansdom ▷ **31** Masterpieces of late Gothic sculpture and baroque altarpieces in this cathedral.

Secession ▷ **56** Landmark building of the Vienna Secession, housing Gustav Klimt's *Beethoven Frieze*.

Schloss Schönbrunn ▷ **99** Summer palace of the Habsburgs with fine gardens and a zoo.

Schloss Belvedere ▷ **82–83** Baroque gardens and two palaces, both housing a core collection of Austrian art.

Rathaus ▷ **55** The neo-Gothic City Hall is the administrative heart of the city and has frequent events on the square in front of it.

Prater and Riesenrad ▷ **98** Amusement park and the Ferris wheel featured in *The Third Man*.

Palais Liechtenstein ▷ **70** A palace housing the Liechtenstein family's art collection.

MuTh ▷ **97** Hear the world's best-known boys' choir in their permanent new home.

These pages are a quick guide to the Top 25, which are described in more detail later. Here they are listed alphabetically, and the tinted background shows which area they are in.

Danube Cruise ▷ 94 Cruises within Vienna and downstream to the Slovak capital, Bratislava.

Freud Museum ▷ 68–69 The home of the founder of psychoanalysis until his emigration in 1938.

Freyung ▷ 25 Baroque palaces and the monastery which gave the square its name.

Heeresgeschichtliches Museum ▷ 80 A military-history museum in a vast complex.

Hofburg ▷ 26–27 The former Imperial Palace was the Habsburg dynasty's residence for six centuries.

Hundertwasser-Haus and KunstHausWien ▷ 95 Postmodern follies designed by Friedensreich Hundertwasser.

Jewish Quarter ▷ 28 One of Vienna's oldest and most historic quarters, centered on Judenplatz.

Kahlenburg ▷ 96 A spur of the Wienerwald with fine views over the city.

Kapuzinergruft ▷ 29 Richly ornate coffins in the Imperial Crypt.

Karlskirche ▷ 81 St. Charles's Church is a masterwork of Fischer von Erlach, father and son.

Kunsthistorisches Museum ▷ 52–53 Famous works by Brueghel and Rubens.

Museum für Angewandte Kunst ▷ 30 Vienna's Museum of Applied Art.

MuseumsQuartier ▷ 54 Exciting district with several museums and interactive spaces.

Shopping

Tracht (traditional costume) is found in shops all over the city. If you don't want to go the whole hog of *Dirndlkleid* or *Lederhosen*, look for the more restrained *Steirer-Jacke* (Styrian jacket with decorative edgings) or the wonderfully enduring Loden overcoats, or even a smart Austrian hat—all of which will still look good when you get home.

Souvenirs and Gifts

Austrians are good at designing charming ornaments, some of which admittedly border on kitsch. Typical are the models of animals and birds made in a variety of different materials. Decorative enamel influenced by the Wiener Werkstätte, the leading producer of which is Michaela Frey, is also attractive, while ladies' purses and handbags embroidered with petit point also make nice presents. Porcelain comes from two great names: Augarten in Vienna and the Gmundner Keramik from Upper Austria. The latter, with its wavy green motifs, is vernacular, while the Augarten is formal and aristocratic.

Local Delicacies

Vienna has plenty of local delicacies—ideal if you are looking for edible gifts to take home. The famous Sachertorte (a chocolate cake invented in 1832) can be shipped anywhere for you from the Sacher shop, likewise the rival *Imperialtorte*. Then there are the Mozart

Christmas shopping; antiques-hunting; Christmas market; clothes boutique; shopping mall (top to bottom)

SHOPPING AREAS

Shopping in the city can roughly be divided into luxury, middle market and cheap. The area comprising Kohlmarkt, Graben and Kärntner Strasse offers chic Austrian goods and international designer labels. Mariahilferstrasse is Vienna's Oxford Street, with the last of the big stores (good for household items and clothing). Cheapest of all is the flea market *(Flohmarkt)* at the west end of the Naschmarkt each Saturday morning. Lots of bargains!

Kugel (gold-wrapped spherical chocolates filled with marzipan and nougat) and the Mozart Thaler (the same, but shaped like coins). These are the trademark Austrian chocolates, but many other *chocolatiers* produce chocolates just as good. Austrian wine remains much underrated (the whites, like Grüner Veltliner or Riesling from the Wachau, are recommended) and the *Sekt* is better than its reputation as the poor man's champagne. *Obstler* (schnapps made from various fruits) is an Austrian specialty much prized by connoisseurs.

Traditional Music

Nothing gives a better taste of a country than its music. A huge selection of CDs of Austrian music (including one-off performances such as the traditional New Year's Eve and New Year concerts of the Vienna Philharmonic at the Musikverein) is on sale in the city. Works by Johann Strauss (the Waltz King) are ubiquitous, as are the indigenous art forms of operetta (Lehár, Kálmán) and *Schrammel* music from the *Heurigen* (taverns). Austrian Broadcasting (ORF) has produced a comprehensive anthology of *Wiener Lieder*, featuring singers like Walter Berry and Angelika Kirchschlager. A fascinating collector's item is the ORF CD of the music of ethnic minorities in Austria, *Hausgemacht*. Music to accompany performances of the Spanish Riding School can be obtained on CD.

MOVING WITH THE TIMES

There was a time when Viennese shopkeepers called all the shots, but much has changed. Despite opposition from retailers, shopping hours have been greatly liberalized: No longer do sad crowds mill around the windows of closed shops on Saturday afternoon; no more do bookstore assistants crouch over the tills, glaring suspiciously at browsers. And for those who want to shop till they drop, there are now several constantly expanding shopping malls. The biggest is the aptly named Shopping City Süd. An alternative is the Ringstrassen Galerien.

Shopping by Theme

Whether you're looking for a department store, a quirky boutique, or something in between, you'll find it in Vienna. On this page, shops are listed by theme. For a more detailed write-up, see the individual listings in Vienna by Area.

Accessories
Alois Frimmel (▷ 87)
Derby-Handschuhe (▷ 38)
Ina Kent Wien (▷ 60)
Köchert (▷ 39)
Modelle-Hüte (▷ 40)
Mühlbauer (▷ 40)
Otto Feiler (▷ 40)
Robert Horn (▷ 40)
Szászi Hüte (▷ 60)

Antiques and Art
C. Bednarczyk (▷ 38)
Dorotheum (▷ 38)
Galerie Ernst Hilger (▷ 39)
Galerie Heike Curtze (▷ 39)
Galerie nächst St. Stephan (▷ 39)
Galerie Nebehay (▷ 39)
Galerie Wolfrum (▷ 39)
Hundertwasser Village (▷ 105)
WOKA (▷ 40)

Books, Maps and Music
Arcadia Opera Shop (▷ 38)
Doblinger (▷ 38)
Freytag & Berndt (▷ 38)
Frick am Graben (▷ 38)
Frick in der Kärntner Strasse (▷ 38)
Hintermayer Büchermarkt (▷ 60)
Rock-Shop (▷ 105)
Shakespeare & Company (▷ 40)

Clothing and Shoes
GEA (▷ 39)
Knize (▷ 39)
Ludwig Reiter (▷ 87)
Mariol (▷ 87)
Tostmann Trachten (▷ 73)

Food and Wine
Altmann & Kühne (▷ 38)
Demmers Teehaus (▷ 73)
Haas & Haas (▷ 39)
Julius Meinl am Graben (▷ 39)
Manner Factory Outlet (▷ 105)
Metzger (▷ 40)
Pischinger (▷ 87)
Schönbichler (▷ 40)
Unger und Klein (▷ 73)
Xocolat Manufaktur (▷ 73)

Glass and China
Augarten (▷ 38)
J. & L. Lobmeyr (▷ 39)
Österreichische Werkstätten (▷ 40)
Wiener Porzellanfabrik (▷ 105)

Interiors
Duft und Kultur (▷ 38)
Rauminhalt (▷ 60)
Wagner Werkhaus (▷ 73)
Wiener Interieur (▷ 40)

Markets
Christkindlmarkt (▷ 60)
Naschmarkt (▷ 60)
Neubaugasse (▷ 60)
Spittelberg Market (▷ 60)

Shopping Malls and Department Stores
BahnhofCity (▷ 87)
Ringstrassengalerien (▷ 60)
Steffl (▷ 40)

Toys
Bader & Partner (▷ 87)
Edi-Bär (▷ 87)
Fürnis Mädchen und Buben (▷ 73)
Pinocchio (▷ 40)

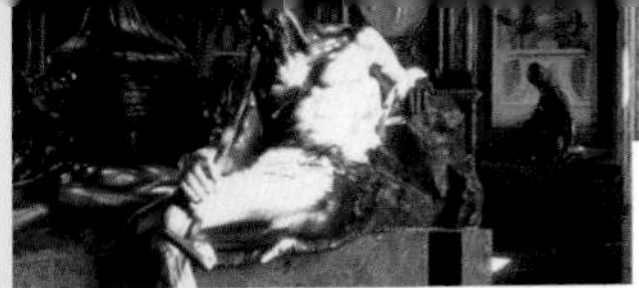

Vienna by Night

Rathaus at dusk; the Blumenrad, in the Prater; Karlskirche illuminated at night (top to bottom)

New *Szenelokale* (trendy or "in" bars and restaurants) open every year in Vienna. These are concentrated in certain areas—the best known is the so-called Bermuda Dreieck (Bermuda Triangle) to the west of Schwedenplatz.

Where to Go

Less self-consciously chic and utterly charming is the Spittelberg area, a good example of inner-city revival. Here you can sit in an 18th-century courtyard, or on a street flanked by baroque and Biedermeier facades, enjoying Austrian regional or ethnic cooking, or check out the many bars and Italian-style cafés. A fun night-time atmosphere has developed in the area from Stephansdom to Am Hof and between Josefstädterstrasse and Laudongasse in the Josefstadt, a region frequented by intellectuals and the well-to-do.

Wine Taverns

An entire culture revolves around the wine taverns of Vienna's peripheral villages, Grinzing, Heiligenstadt, Salmannsdorf and Neustift am Walde being the best known. You may prefer this to the bustle of the city; here you can sip white wine in the peace of a *Heuriger* (▷ 106) garden and tuck into a *Heuriger* pork roast.

Floodlit Monuments

Perhaps the greatest evening pleasure is entirely free, namely walking around the floodlit monuments of the Inner City.

BALMY EVENINGS

Exploiting five and a half months of mild to warm weather, in Vienna you can linger at café or restaurant tables on the sidewalk outside, or in *Heurigen* gardens, until late into the evening. A restaurant extension is known as a *Schanigarten*, from the nickname of the first person to erect one on the Graben in 1754. In summer there are also major open-air events, among them the jazz festival on the Donauinsel and the opera films in front of the Rathaus.

Eating Out

The general standard of Viennese cuisine is high, even at the cheaper end of the market. The Nordsee chain offers very acceptable fast-food fish dishes and there is a broad range of middle-price *gute bürgerliche Küche* (good bourgeois cuisine). But gourmets will not go hungry either.

Ethnic Influences

Vienna's kitchen has always been a mixture of Austrian recipes and those of its Central European neighbors, formerly part of the Habsburg Empire. The famous Wiener schnitzel is derived from the *scaloppina Milanese* from Lombardy, goulash was imported from Hungary, and some Bohemian dishes (chiefly various kinds of dumplings) have survived here, even when they are now hard to find in the Czech lands. Over the past decade, an invasion of the Turkish doner kebab has followed the pizza wave, although this is more a feature of the suburbs than the main tourist areas.

Run the Gamut from Beef to Ice Cream

Austria is a land-locked country and Vienna's cooking has always focused on meat and cereals. Beef (especially boiled beef, called *Tafelspitz*) has a long tradition in the city; in a few restaurants that concentrate on it, the variety of beef dishes is amazing. Everything depends upon the quality of the beef itself, as well as careful preparation and fresh condiments, if the real *Tafelspitz* experience is to be enjoyed. Moving from the savory to the sweet, Vienna's ice-cream salons have a selection and quality to rival those of Italy.

THAT UNIQUE LOCAL EXPERIENCE

Specific to Vienna are the *Heurigen* (wine taverns) on the outskirts of the city. In the old town of the inner city, there are also deep wine cellars, sometimes descending two levels through baroque to Gothic foundations. Above ground in summer, you can lunch in one of the popular garden restaurants or dine in a princely palace.

Viennese cakes and pastries—especially the famous Sachertorte—can be enjoyed in the city's coffeehouses

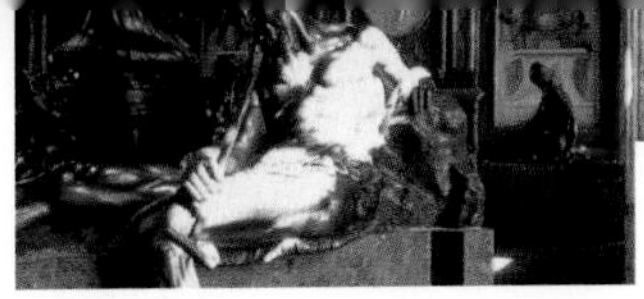

Restaurants by Cuisine

There are restaurants to suit all tastes and budgets in Vienna. On this page they are listed by cuisine. For a more detailed description of each restaurant, see Vienna by Area.

Asian
Akakiko (▷ 62)
Green Cottage (▷ 62)

Beisl
Beim Czaak (▷ 43)
Glacis Beisl (panel, ▷ 54)
Kern's Beisl (▷ 45)
Restaurant Wiener (▷ 63)

Cellars
Esterhazykeller (▷ 44)
Piaristenkeller (▷ 62)
Rathauskeller (▷ 63)
Salm Bräu (▷ 89)

Coffeehouses and Cafés
Aida (▷ 43)
Berg (▷ 75)
Café Bräunerhof (▷ 24)
Café Central (▷ 43)
Café Diglas (▷ 43)
Café Drechsler (▷ 62)
Café Eiles (▷ 62)
Café Landtmann (▷ 62)
Café Leopold Hawelka (▷ 24)
Café Prückel (▷ 43)
Café Sacher (▷ 43)
Café Schwarzenberg (▷ 62)
Café Sperl (▷ 62)
Demel (▷ 44)
Dommayer (▷ 106)
Heiner (▷ 44)

Heurigen
Fuhrgassl-Huber (▷ 106)
Mayer am Pfarrplatz (▷ 106)
Zimmermann (▷ 106)

International
Bodega Española (▷ 89)
Do & Co (▷ 44)
Ethiopian Restaurant (▷ 75)
Restaurant Lale (▷ 45)

Italian
Casa Alberto (▷ 89)
Fabios (▷ 44)
La Pasteria (▷ 75)

Seafood
Kornat (▷ 45)
Ragusa (▷ 75)

Vegetarian
Wrenkh (▷ 45)

Vienna's Best
At Eight (▷ 43)
Bristol Lounge (▷ 43)
Le Ciel (▷ 43)
Donauturm (▷ 106)
Hollmann Salon (▷ 45)
Holy-Moly! (▷ 45)
Plachutta (▷ 45, 106)
Das Schick (▷ 63)
Sluka (▷ 63)
Steirereck (▷ 89)

Viennese/Austrian
Figlmüller (▷ 44)
Haas & Haas (▷ 44)
Klein Steiermark (▷ 89)
Meinl am Graben (▷ 45)
Porzellan (▷ 75)
Roth (▷ 75)
Schnattl (▷ 63)
Servitenwirt (▷ 75)
Sperl (▷ 89)
Stadtpark Bräu (▷ 89)
Wild (▷ 106)
Zu ebener Erde und erster Stock (▷ 63)

Top Tips For...

These great suggestions will help you tailor your ideal visit to Vienna, no matter how you choose to spend your time. Each sight or listing has a fuller write-up elsewhere in the book.

CLASSICAL MUSIC

Practice your conducting in the Haus der Musik (▷ 33).
Savor the musicianship of the Wiener Philharmoniker in the Golden Hall of the Musikverein (▷ 88).
Pay homage to Mozart at the Mozarthaus (▷ 34), where he once lodged.

Musikverein (top); cakes galore in Vienna's coffeehouses (above)

COFFEEHOUSES

Order the original Sachertorte at Café Sacher (▷ 43), in the celebrated Hotel Sacher—or have it mailed to friends from the Sacher shop.
Meet friends at Café Landtmann (▷ 62).
Indulge yourself at Demel patisserie (▷ 44), a former purveyor to the imperial household.

ANTIQUES SHOPPING

Buy Augarten porcelain (▷ 38) decorated with floral designs in the former Augarten Palace, now a factory for this famous ware.
Consult the experts on Secessionist art at Christian Nebehay's gallery/shop (▷ 39).
Bid at an auction at "Aunt Dorothy" (Dorotheum, ▷ 38), Vienna's traditional auction house.

CLOTHES AND ACCESSORIES

Have a gentleman's suit made for you at Knize's shop (▷ 39).
Splash out on a luxurious handbag at Ina Kent Wien (▷ 60).
Check out the headgear at Szászi Hüte—a hat for every occasion (▷ 60).

Shop for antiques (above right) or that perfect hat (right)

e Ankeruhr (below); ·tel Imperial ·nter)

WHAT'S FREE

Enjoy music films on a huge screen in front of the Rathaus (July and August, ▷ 55).

Walk to or from the Kahlenberg through woods and vineyards (▷ 96).

Watch the figures of the Ankeruhr move across the clockface at noon (▷ 28).

HOTELS WITH CHARACTER

Enjoy a cutting-edge hotel experience at the slick Do & Co (▷ 112).

Indulge your love of wine at the unique Hotel Rathaus Wine and Design (▷ 111).

Combine Viennese tradition with modern comfort at Hotel Sacher (▷ 112).

Mingle with kings and presidents at Hotel Imperial (▷ 112), used as official accommodations for state visitors.

ATMOSPHERIC RESTAURANTS

Enjoy the food in the cavernous interior of the Rathaus at the Rathauskeller (▷ 63).

Soak in the atmosphere of the Austro-Hungarian monarchy in the Piaristenkeller (▷ 62).

Eat in a traditional *Beisl*, such as Beim Czaak (▷ 43).

Eat or drink in a Viennese cellar or Beisl *(above)*

NIGHTLIFE

Join an evening roof walk of St. Stephen's Cathedral (▷ 31).

Meet Vienna's high society at the exclusive Eden Bar (▷ 41).

Get fired up with local and international DJs at Flex, beside the Danube Canal (▷ 61).

St. Stephen's Cathedral after dark (left)

The Secession (below); riding the Ferris wheel in the Prater (center)

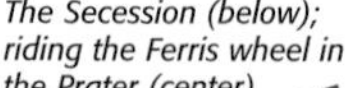

AUSTRIAN SECESSION AND EXPRESSIONISTS

Be sure to see the "Golden Cabbage" on top of the Secession (▷ 56)—and the *Beethoven Frieze* in the Secession basement.
Don't miss the paintings by Klimt, Schiele and Kokoschka at the gallery in the Upper Belvedere (▷ 82).
Look inside Otto Wagner's Postsparkassenamt (▷ 34) for its dazzling white hall.
Join a guided tour of Wagner's Kirche am Steinhof (▷ 100), which combines functionalism with beauty.

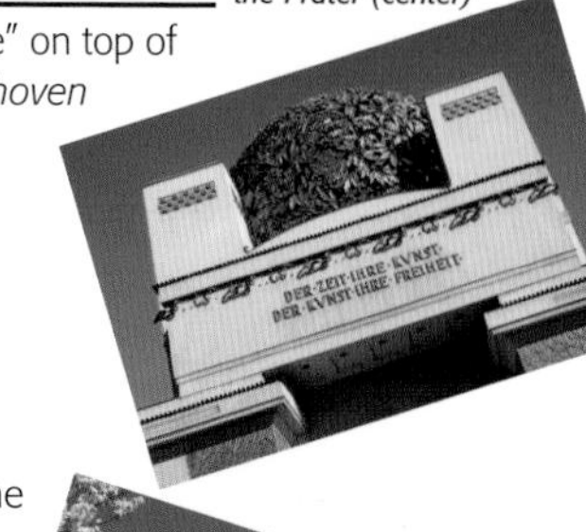

CHILDREN'S ACTIVITIES

Ride the Ferris wheel and try some of the other attractions in the Prater (▷ 98).
Take a boat tour of the Seegrotte in Hinterbrühl (▷ 104), Europe's largest underground lake.
Get lost in the baroque labyrinth of the park at Schloss Schönbrunn (▷ 99).

SHOE-STRING ACCOMMODATIONS

Arrive home at the Time Out City Hotel (▷ 109) to enjoy family-style comfort in Jugendstil opulence.
Save money by staying in one of the city's many private rooms (▷ 109).

Even visitors on a budget will find inexpensive accommodations (above)

LUXURY LIVING

Order a bottle of wine and relax at Le Ciel (▷ 43), on the top floor of the Grand Hotel Wien.
Splash out on handmade shoes by top shoemaker Ludwig Reiter (▷ 87).
Dine in the glassed terrace of Fabios, Vienna's authentic Italian eatery (▷ 44).

Splashing out on wine (right)

Vienna by Area

St. Stephen's Cathedral and the imperial palace of the Hofburg are the highlights of Vienna's ancient and historic heart, but everywhere in the Innere Stadt you will encounter the entire palette of architectural styles and curiosities.

Freyung
INNERE STADT
Esperanto Museum
Globenmuseum
Holocaust Memorial
Jewish Quarter
Uhrenmuseum
Peterskirche
Artaria Haus
Coffeehouses
Hofburg
Augustinerkirche
Albertina
Burggarten
Donner Brunnen
Kapuzinergruft
Lobkowitz-Palais
Annakirche
Haus der Musik
Staatsoper
Karlsplatz Pavilions
Resselpark
Karlsplatz
OPERNRING
KÄRNTNER RING
FRANZ-JOSEF
Donaukanal
0
250 m
0
250 yds
2
3
4
5
6
D
E
F

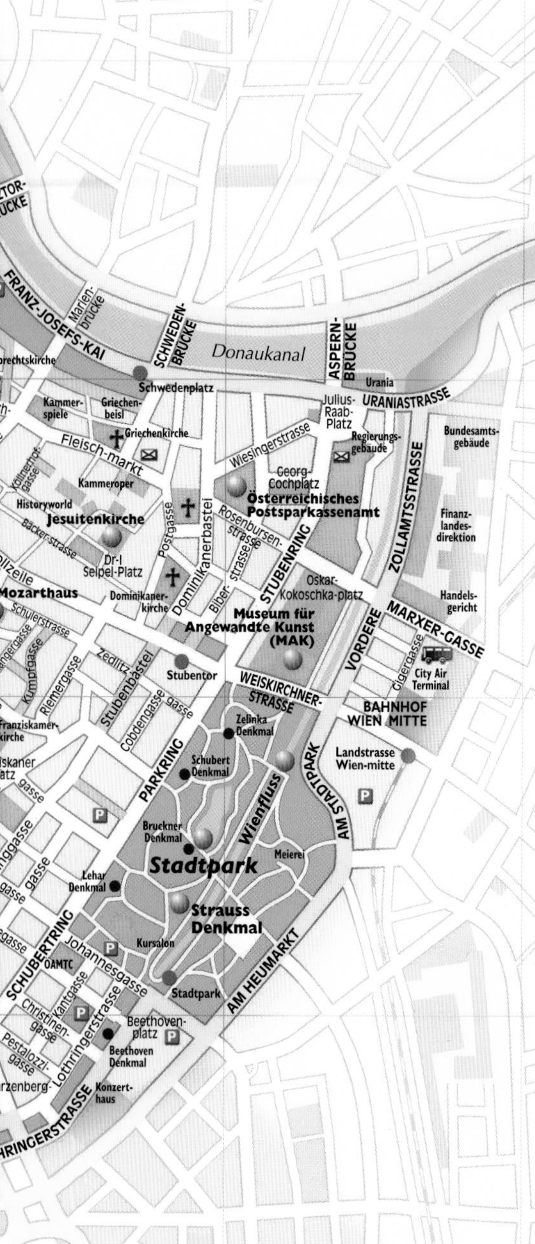

FRANZ-JOSEFS-KAI
Marienbrücke
SCHWEDENBRÜCKE
Donaukanal
ASPERNBRÜCKE
Urania
URANIASTRASSE
Schwedenplatz
Kammerspiele
Griechenbeisl
Griechenkirche
Fleisch-markt
Kammeroper
Historyworld
Jesuitenkirche
Bäcker-strasse
Dr-I Seipel-Platz
Postgasse
Dominikanerbastei
Dominikanerkirche
Rosenbursenstrasse
Biberstrasse
Wiesingerstrasse
Julius-Raab-Platz
Regierungsgebäude
Georg-Cochplatz
Österreichisches Postsparkassenamt
STUBENRING
ZOLLAMTSSTRASSE
Bundesamtsgebäude
Finanzlandesdirektion
Handelsgericht
Oskar-Kokoschka-platz
Mozarthaus
Schulerstrasse
Museum für Angewandte Kunst (MAK)
VORDERE
MARXER-GASSE
Gigergasse
City Air Terminal
Kumpfgasse
Riemergasse
Zedlitzgasse
Stubenbastei
Cobdengasse
Stubentor
WEISKIRCHNER-STRASSE
BAHNHOF WIEN MITTE
Landstrasse Wien-mitte
Franziskanerkirche
Zelinka Denkmal
Schubert Denkmal
PARKRING
Wienfluss
AM STADTPARK
Bruckner Denkmal
Meierei
Stadtpark
Lehar Denkmal
Strauss Denkmal
SCHUBERTRING
Kursalon
Johannesgasse
OAMTC
Kantgasse
Christinengasse
Lothringerstrasse
Stadtpark
AM HEUMARKT
Beethovenplatz
Beethoven Denkmal
Pestalozzigasse
Konzerthaus
LOTHRINGERSTRASSE
G
H

Coffeehouses

TOP 25

Linger in a coffeehouse and enjoy the atmosphere as well as the coffee and cakes

THE BASICS

Café Bräunerhof
www.braeunerhof.at
F5
Stallburggasse 2
512 38 93
Daily 8am–8.30pm
U1, U3 to Stephansdom
Moderate

Café Leopold Hawelka
www.hawelka.at
F4
Dorotheergasse 6
512 82 30
Mon–Sat 8am–midnight, Sun 10am–midnight
U1, U3 to Stephansdom
Inexpensive

TIP

- Coffeehouses serve more than just coffee. You can almost always get beer or wine, decent traditional Austrian food, and, of course, ice cream and cakes. They also have newspapers and magazines lying around for their customers' enjoyment.

Coffeehouses are an integral part of Vienna's culture. They function as public living rooms or lounges; places to meet friends, grab a meal or quick bite, or merely take a solitary coffee break.

History Legend has it that coffee first came to Vienna via the Turks during their siege of the city in the late 17th century. By the 19th century, the Wiener Kaffeehaus—with its trademark *grand salons* and stuffy waiters—was firmly entrenched on the local scene. The list of *stammgäste* (regulars) to Vienna's coffeehouses over the years reads like a Who's Who of Central European luminaries—from Vladimir Lenin to Sigmund Freud.

Protocol Coffeehouses are usually relaxed affairs, but it helps to know a few rules. The first concerns which coffee to order. The four most common ones are: *Kleiner schwarzer* (small black coffee, similar to espresso); *Kleiner brauner* (espresso with a shot of milk); *Verlängerter* (means "stretched" in German, hot water added to espresso like an Americano); and *Melange* (a *Verlängerter* with foamed milk, like a cappuccino).

Where to find them Just about every neighborhood in the city has a classic coffeehouse, but most tend to be in the Innere Stadt and around the Ringstrasse. Two popular ones in the Innere Stadt are Café Bräunerhof and Café Leopold Hawelka.

Detail of Kinsky-Palais (left); Kinsky-Palais (middle); clock tower of Schottenkirche (right)

TOP 25 Freyung

This irregularly shaped square acquired its name (meaning "asylum") due to the adjacent Benedictine monastery, which until 1848 had the right to give asylum to fugitives from justice.

Freyung Eighteenth-century Canaletto paintings show a lively scene, with stall vendors, jugglers and clowns. Baroque palaces still rim the square.

Schottenkirche The Abbey Church of the "Schotten" Benedictines, dominating the east side of the square, was called Scottish because the Latin name for Ireland was *Scotia maior*. The 15th-century Gothic altarpiece, now in the Museum im Schottenstift in the Schottenkirche, shows the earliest extant view of Vienna.

Palais Ferstel This structure is not actually a palace but a complex named after its architect. Inside, a glass-roofed arcade lined with gift shops leads from the Freyung to Herrengasse ("Street of the Lords"). It was formerly the seat of the Vienna Stock Exchange.

Kinsky-Palais This is one of Lukas von Hildebrandt's masterworks and was built in 1716, with a slim, elegant facade that overlooks the Freyung. Try to get a look at the ceremonial staircase inside and also its ceiling fresco, *Apotheosis of a War Hero*, which flatters Count Philipp von Daun, the military commander who first owned the palace.

THE BASICS

E3

Schottenkirche and Museum im Schottenstift: Freyung 6. Palais Ferstel: Freyung 2

Schottenkirche: 534 98-200. Museum: 534 98 600

Schottenkirche: usually daily 7am–9pm. Museum: Thu–Fri 11–5, Sat 11–4.30

Café Central in Palais Ferstel (▷ 43)

U2 to Schottentor, U3 to Herrengasse

Hopper I

Few

Inexpensive

HIGHLIGHTS

Freyung

- Medieval cobbles in the northeast corner
- Hildebrandt's Kinsky-Palais, Freyung 4

Schottenkirche and Schottenstift Museum

- Gothic wing altar, Master of the Scots 1469–80
- High altar (Ferstel)
- Tomb of Count Starhemberg

Palais Ferstel

- Danube Fountain

Hofburg

TOP 25

HIGHLIGHTS

- Imperial Treasury
- Imperial Apartments with Silver Collection
- Court Chapel and Vienna Boys' Choir
- Spanish Riding School
- Prunksaal of the National Library

TIP

- After a trip to the Spanish Riding School, continue the equestrian theme by picking up a horse-drawn carriage in Heldenplatz.

It is said that the Habsburgs never finished their great projects; the Hofburg (the former imperial residence), like St. Stephen's Cathedral (▷ 31) and the Habsburg Empire itself, is an example of their unfinished business.

Traditions In terms of history, the Hofburg (the Habsburg residence) is more significant than all other buildings in Vienna. It houses secular and sacred treasuries (Schatzkammer) containing the crowns of the Holy Roman Empire and of the Empire of Austria. Three institutions still operate in the Hofburg: the Hofmusikkapelle (Court Music Chapel), where the Wiener Sängerknaben (Vienna Boys' Choir) sing Sunday Mass in the Burgkapelle (Court Chapel; mid-Sep to Jun); the Spanische Hofreitschule

Clockwise from far left: Equestrian statue of Prince Eugene of Savoy in Heroes Square; statue on the Neue Hofburg; eagle above St. Michael's Gate; imperial plate in the Sisi Museum; Imperial Apartments in the Sisi Museum

(Spanish Riding School), a center of equestrian excellence famed for its dancing horses; and the Nationalbibliothek (National Library).

Architecture The earliest fortress here was built in 1275 on the site that became the Schweizerhof (Swiss Court), named after the former Swiss Guard. The Schweizerhof incorporates the Gothic Burgkapelle and the Renaissance Schweizertor (Swiss Gate). There were baroque extensions of the original Hofburg. The Neue Hofburg, partially framing the Heldenplatz (Heroes Square) was built in Historicist style and completed on the eve of World War I. On the square are the equestrian statues of Prince Eugene of Savoy (hero of the Turkish Wars) and Archduke Charles (victor of the Battle of Aspern against Napoleon).

THE BASICS

www.hofburg-wien.at
www.hofmusikkapelle.gv.at
www.srs.at

E5

Imperial Apartments, Sisi Museum, Silver and Tableware Collection: Hofburg—Michaelerkuppel; Nationalbibliothek: Josefplatz 1; Burgkapelle: Hofburg—Schweizerhof

Imperial Apartments, Sisi Museum, Silver and Tableware Collection: 533 75 70; Nationalbibliothek: 534 10-0; Burgkapelle: 533 99 27

Imperial Apartments, Sisi Museum, Silver and Tableware Collection: daily 9–5.30 (Jul–Aug 9–6). Guided tours daily 2pm; Treasury: Wed–Mon 10–6; Burgkapelle: Mass mid-Sep to Jun Sun 9.15, reservation needed; Riding School: morning training (with music) daily 10–noon, performances Sat–Sun 11 (tickets from visitor center at Michaelerplatz 1), summer and winter break guided tours daily 2, 3 and 4 (reservations tel: 533 90 31); Prunksaal of the National Library: Tue–Sun 10–6, Thu 10–9

U3 to Herrengasse

Bus 2A, 3A to Hofburg

Few; good for library

Expensive

Jewish Quarter

The Ankeruhr on Hoher Markt (left); the Holocaust Memorial on Judenplatz (right)

THE BASICS

F3

Stadttempel

www.jmw.at

Seitenstettengasse 4

535 04 31-33

By guided tour only: Mon–Thu 11.30, 2. Closed public hols

U1, U4 to Schwedenplatz

Bus 3A to Hoher Markt; tram 1 to Schwedenplatz

Excellent

Inexpensive

Jüdisches Museum Wien

www.jmw.at

Misrachi Haus, Judenplatz 8

535 04 31-213

Sun–Thu 10–6, Fri 10–2

U1, U3 to Stephansplatz

Bus 3A to Hoher Markt

Excellent

Inexpensive

Jüdisches Museum Wien/Dorotheergasse

Dorotheergasse 11

535 04 31

Sun–Fri 10–6

U1, U3 to Stephansplatz

Excellent

Inexpensive

Vienna's historic Jewish Quarter has two focal points: the old Stadttempel and the modern Holocaust Memorial. Today's Jewish community is northeast of the Danube Canal.

Stadttempel Hidden behind a simple facade, the neoclassical synagogue in Seitenstettengasse is the only place of Jewish worship that survived the Nazi pogroms in Vienna. The offices of the Jewish community and other institutions are in the building.

Hoher Markt and Altes Rathaus En route from Judengasse to Judenplatz you cross Hoher Markt. At its northeast corner is the famous Ankeruhr (Franz von Matsch, 1913). Every hour a different figure from Austrian history revolves around the clock face, while at noon all the figures appear in sequence. The former City Hall (Altes Rathaus) in Wipplingerstrasse is overshadowed by the mighty facade of the former Bohemian Court Chancellery across the street.

Holocaust Memorial Judenplatz was the heart of the medieval ghetto. Remains of a synagogue can be seen beneath the Jewish Museum at Misrachi Haus, while the square is dominated by Rachel Whiteread's Holocaust Memorial, which remembers the 65,000 Austrian Jews killed in World War II. A branch of the Jewish Museum, on Dorotheergasse, focuses on contemporary Jewish life in Vienna.

Imperial tombs (left); a macabre detail of Karl VI's tomb in the Capuchin Crypt (right)

TOP 25

Kapuzinergruft

Deceased emperors' hearts are preserved in the Augustinian Church (▷ 32), their embalmed entrails in St. Stephen's (▷ 31) and their bodies here in the Capuchin Crypt, a shrine for pilgrims and loyalists.

The Capuchins and their church The Franciscan Capuchins came to Austria in the reign of Duke (later Emperor) Matthias (1612–19), whose wife, Empress Anna, founded their monastery in 1618. The preacher Marco d'Aviano was Vienna's most celebrated Capuchin. Famously intrepid, he went into battle with the imperial forces against the Turkish army, which was besieging Vienna in 1683. He is buried in one of the church's chapels.

Simplicity The building is in accord with the austere precepts of the Capuchins. Almost the only decoration is a 1936 fresco of St. Francis of Assisi and a cross on the facade. Inside is the Kaiserkapelle (Emperor Chapel), with wooden statues of emperors Matthias and Ferdinand II, III and IV. The Chapel of the Cross has an altar by Lukas von Hildebrandt and a very moving pietà (Mary embracing the dead Christ).

Habsburg resting place The first emperor and empress to be buried in the crypt were Matthias and his wife Anna. Since then 138 members of the Habsburg family have been interred here, along with Maria Theresa's governess. The simple copper coffin of Joseph II is a reminder of its occupant's distaste for religious excess.

THE BASICS

www.kaisergruft.at
F5
Tegetthoffstrasse 2
512 6853-16
Daily 10–6. Closed 1, 2 Nov
U1, U3 to Stephansplatz
Bus 3A to Albertinaplatz
Good
Church free; crypt inexpensive

HIGHLIGHTS

The church
- Bronze of Marco d'Aviano
- Statues of four emperors
- Marble altar by Hildebrandt
- Pietà, by Peter Strudel and Matthias Steinl

The crypt
- Tomb of Charles IV
- Double tomb of Franz Stephan and Maria Theresa
- Tombs of Franz Joseph and Elisabeth
- Bust of the last emperor, Karl, and coffin of the last empress, Zita

Museum für Angewandte Kunst (MAK)

Chair (left) and graphic (middle) by Josef Hoffmann; vase by the Wiener Werkstätte (right)

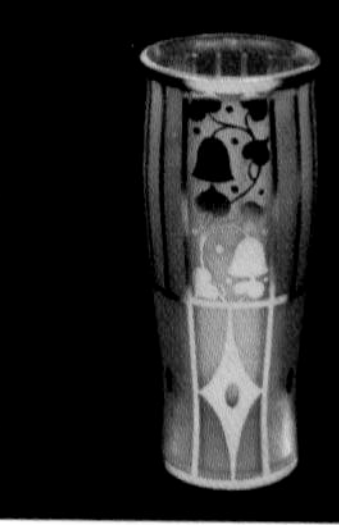

THE BASICS

www.mak.at

H4

Stubenring 5

711 360; recorded information 711 36-248

Tue 10–10, Wed–Sun 10–6. Closed 1 May, 1 Nov, 24, 25, 31 Dec

Elegant café

Schnellbahn to Landstrasse

U3 to Stubentor, U4 to Landstrasse-Wien Mitte

Tram 2 to Stubentor

Good

Moderate; free admission Sat

Guided tours in English Sun at noon. Frequent special exhibitions

HIGHLIGHTS

- Atrium
- 16th-century Egyptian silk carpet
- 15th-century Buddha head
- Meissen bear
- Bohemian glass
- Lobmeyr glass (Vienna)

A striking example of minimalist display techniques at the Museum of Applied Art is the projection of silhouettes of chairs against a white screen, which emphasizes the beauty of the designs.

Forerunner Established in 1864, the MAK was the first museum of its kind in Europe. The initiative came from art historian Rudolf Eitelberger, who had been much impressed by London's South Kensington Museum, later the Victoria and Albert Museum.

Decorative The 1871 neo-Renaissance building by Heinrich Ferstel combines architecture with applied art—its facade is ornamented with sgraffito and majolica portrait medallions of artist-craftsmen.

The interior The entrance leads to a beautiful atrium, with arcades around each floor. In contrast, a glass-and-steel passageway connects different parts of the building.

The collections The amazingly rich collections include a fine selection of Jugendstil, Biedermeier and Thonet furniture from Austria. There is a section devoted to objects from the East (textiles, carpets and ceramics), and another part contains European decorative art, including both Venetian and Bohemian glass, Meissen porcelain, and jewelry. The display of works by leading artists of the Wiener Werkstätte on the first floor alone is worth the visit.

Elaborately carved pulpit in the cathedral (left); the striking tiled roof (right)

TOP 25

Stephansdom

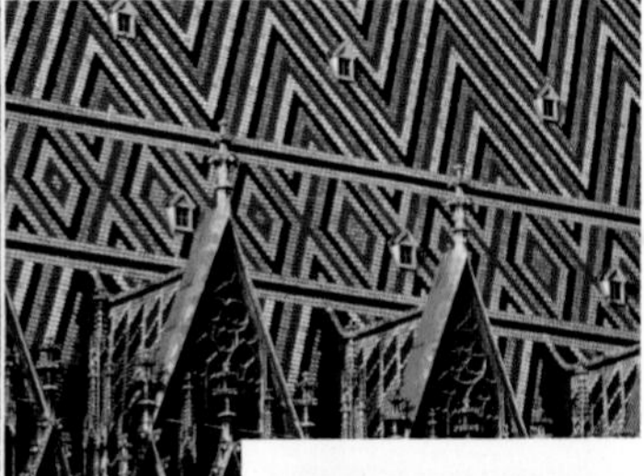

St. Stephen's Cathedral has been the spiritual focus of the Viennese people since the Middle Ages—its massive Pummerin Bell rings in the New Year. The great South Tower is affectionately known as the Steffl ("Little Steve").

Ornamentation From the three preceding Romanesque churches on this site, only the Giant's Door and Heathen Towers (so called because a pagan shrine was supposed to have been here) have survived as part of the Gothic church. Note the striking yellow, green and black chevrons of the tiled roof and a representation of the Habsburg double-headed eagle. Against the north external wall is the pulpit marking the spot where Giovanni Capistrano (1386–1456) preached fiery sermons against the Turks. The cathedral is considered a symbol of endurance, having undergone numerous repairs due to the ravages of the Turks, the Napoleonic French and the Allies. All the Federal States contributed to the cathedral's restoration after World War II.

Inside Anton Pilgram's late Gothic pulpit with portraits of the fathers of the church is near the entrance. Above the organ loft of the north aisle is a sculpted self-portrait of Pilgram holding a square and compass. The Gothic vaulting in the Albertine Choir is especially beautiful. Tobias Pock's 1647 baroque altar painting shows the martyrdom of St. Stephen. In the north apse is the Wiener Neustädter Altar (1447). In the south apse is the marble tomb of Friedrich III.

THE BASICS

www.stephanskirche.at
F4
Stephansplatz 3
51 552-3054
Church, catacombs, treasury and bell tower: Mon–Sat 9–11.30, 1–4.30; Sun 1–4.30. South tower: daily 9–5.30
U1, U3 to Stephansplatz
Buses 1A, 2A
Main church: good
Church: free; choir: moderate (guided tour only); catacombs, bell tower, treasury, south tower: inexpensive; combined ticket: expensive
Evening tours in English Jun–Sep Sat 7pm (meet at south tower reception, moderate)

HIGHLIGHTS

- Pilgram's pulpit
- Tomb of Prince Eugene of Savoy, Kreuzkapelle
- Pummerin Bell
- Nicolas van Leyden's tomb of Friedrich III (1440–93)

More to See

ALBERTINA

www.albertina.at

Louis Montoyer built this gallery between 1801 and 1804 to house the magnificent collection of artworks assembled by Duke Albert of Sachsen-Teschen. The Albertina is the world's leading graphic collection, comprising more than a million items. Its famous drawings and etchings are kept in controlled conditions to preserve them and are seldom on display, because light would damage their fragile structure.

F5 Albertinaplatz 1 534 83-0 Daily 10–6, Wed 10–9 U1, U2, U4 to Karlsplatz, U3 to Stephansplatz Bus 3A to Albertinaplatz Good Moderate Tours: audio guide in English

ANNAKIRCHE

www.annakirche.at

An intimate gem of early 17th-century baroque architecture, with Daniel Gran's ceiling fresco of the Immaculate Conception. In the side chapel is a beautiful Gothic carving of Mary, Jesus and St. Anne by Veit Stoss of Nürnberg.

F5 Annagasse 3B 512 47 97 Daily 9–12, 2.30–5.30 U1, U3 to Stephansplatz

Annakirche

ARTARIA HAUS

Max Fabiani's Artaria House is one of the most striking Jugendstil buildings in the city.

F4 Kohlmarkt 9 U3 to Herrengasse

AUGUSTINERKIRCHE

www.augustinerkirche.at

The Church of St. Augustine, the parish church of the Habsburg court, can seem forbidding from the exterior. In its Loreto Chapel are preserved the hearts of members of the imperial family. On Sunday Vienna's best-sung Masses cheer things up.

F5 Augustinerstrasse 3 (entrance Josefsplatz) 533 70 99 Mon–Sat 7.30–7.30, Sun 1–6, sung Mass Sep–Jun Sun 11 U1, U2, U4 to Karlsplatz/Oper, U3 to Herrengasse Hopper 3A to Albertinaplatz Church only Inexpensive Tour of Loreto Chapel and Herzgruft after Mass Sun

BURGGARTEN

www.palmenhaus.at

The vast Jugendstil glasshouse built by Friedrich Ohmann in 1907 now houses a restaurant and bars.

E5 Opernring Mar–Oct daily 10am–2am; Nov–Feb Mon–Thu 11.30am–midnight, Fri–Sat 10am–1am, Sun 10am–midnight. Closed Mon–Tue in Jan–Feb Trams 1, 2, D to Burgring

DONNER BRUNNEN

This is a copy of Georg Raphael Donner's Providentia Fountain, which stands in the Belvedere

(▷ 82–83). Maria Theresa disapproved of the nude figures. The water nymphs symbolize the rivers of Lower Austria.
F5 Neuer Markt U1, U3 to Stephansplatz

ESPERANTO MUSEUM
www.onb.at
A unique collection featuring invented languages. It covers everything from philosophical considerations to terminology, the planning of new languages and intervention in existing ones.
E4 Palais Mollard 534 10-730 Tue–Wed, Fri–Sun 10–6, Thu 10–9 U3 to Herrengasse Good Inexpensive

GLOBENMUSEUM
www.onb.at
The historic globes in the collection of the Austrian National Library (in the same building as the Esperanto Museum, above) are unique. The oldest one dates back to 1536, but the most precious items are the 10 globes by Venetian Vicenzo Coronelli from the late 17th century. There are also globes featuring the moon and the planets.
E4 Mollard Palace, Herrengasse 9 534 10-710 Tue–Wed, Fri–Sun 10–6, Thu 10–9 Good Inexpensive

HAUS DER MUSIK
www.hausdermusik.at
The approach at Vienna's sound museum is practical and participatory, so visitors get to compose their own waltz, conduct, or play instruments. It is certainly a far cry from musty exhibits in glass cases. There's also a good restaurant.
F5 Seilerstätte 30 513 48 50 Daily 10–10 U1, U2, U4 to Karlsplatz Trams D, 2 to Schwarzenbergplatz Good Moderate; combined ticket with Mozarthaus (▷ 34)

JESUITENKIRCHE
www.jesuiten.at
Italian-born Andrea Pozzo, a Jesuit brother, designed this beautiful, ornate church in the early 18th

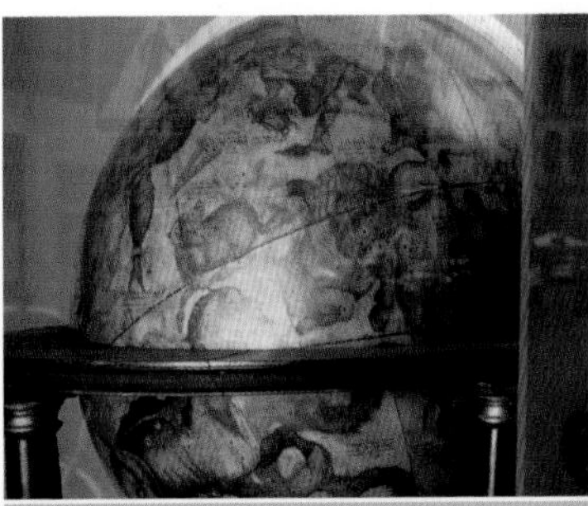
An exhibit in the Globenmuseum

Donner Fountain

century. It belonged to the adjacent university, over which the Jesuits gained control in 1622. From this base the Jesuits drove forward the Counter-Reformation in Vienna.

G4 Dr-Ignaz-Seipel-Platz 1 512 52 32-0 Daily 7am–6pm U3 to Stubentor

KARLSPLATZ PAVILIONS

Architect Otto Wagner designed the City Transit Railway. The finest stations are the two on Karlsplatz (1898) and the emperor's own at Schönbrunn. One of the Karlsplatz pavilions houses a museum dedicated to the architect.

F6 Karlsplatz Museum: Tue–Sun 10–6. Closed 1 Nov–31 Mar U1, U2, U4 to Karlsplatz Museum: inexpensive; free first Sun of month

LOBKOWITZ-PALAIS

www.theatermuseum.at

The present impressive facade is by Johann Bernhard Fischer von Erlach. Beethoven's Eroica Symphony was first performed here in 1804, and during the Congress of Vienna many famous balls were held. The Austrian Theater Museum is here, hosting temporary exhibitions.

F5 Lobkowitzplatz 2 525 24-3460 Wed–Mon 10–6 U1, U2, U4 to Karlsplatz/Oper Moderate

MOZARTHAUS

www.mozarthausvienna.at

Visit Mozart's lodgings where he wrote *The Marriage of Figaro*. No contemporary furniture has survived, but there is a vivid and entertaining presentation of his life and times. The audio guide includes examples of his music.

G4 Domgasse 5 512 17 91 Daily 10–7 Café on premises U1, U3 to Stephansplatz Good Moderate. Combined ticket includes Haus der Musik (▷ 33) Museum shop

ÖSTERREICHISCHES POSTSPARKASSENAMT

The functionalism of Otto Wagner's Austrian Post Office Savings Bank

Otto Wagner's Pavilions on Karlsplatz

Mozarthaus

(built between 1910 and 1912) made it seem ahead of its time. While it continues to operate as a bank, it also has a small museum dedicated to Otto Wagner.

H4 Georg-Coch-Platz 534 53-33088 Mon–Fri 9–5, Sat 10–5 U1, U4 to Schwedenplatz Trams 1, 2 to Julius-Raab-Platz Moderate

PETERSKIRCHE

www.peterskirche.at

The most striking aspect of the lovely baroque St. Peter's Church is the way the architects, Gabriele Montani and Lukas von Hildebrandt, fitted it into a space so narrow that it looks almost as if it had been poured into a mold.

F4 Petersplatz 6 533 64 33 Mon–Fri 7–7, Sat–Sun 9–7 U1, U3 to Stephansplatz Hopper 2A Few Free

STAATSOPER

www.wiener-staatsoper.at

The State Opera, which closed in 1944, reopened in 1955 with a performance of Beethoven's *Fidelio*. It remains one of the world's top opera stages.

F5 Opernring 2 51 444-2250, 51 444-2614 tours Entrance by guided tour only. Tours in English at 2 and 3 U1, U2, U4 to Oper

Strauss Monument

STADTPARK

Laid out in 1863 on the old River Wien causeway, the park is packed with monuments to the composers and artists of 19th-century Vienna.

G5 Stubenring Daily 8am–dusk U3 to Stubentor, U4 to Stadtpark

STRAUSS DENKMAL

The famous statue of the Viennese Waltz King (▷ picture, below).

G5 Stadtpark Tram 2 to Weihburggasse

UHRENMUSEUM

www.wienmuseum.at

The first of its kind in the world, the Clock Museum covers three floors of the Obizzi Palace and houses more than 3,000 exhibits from the 15th to the 20th centuries. Many are unique, including the "zappler"–a tiny clock that can be covered with a thimble.

F4 Schulhof 2 (alley flanking Am Hof church) 533 22 65 Tue–Sun 10–6 U1, U3 to Stephansplatz Hopper 2A None Inexpensive; free first Sun of month Tours

WIENFLUSS

Just behind the Strauss Monument, the River Wien leaves its covered channel and emerges through a Secessionist framework designed by Friedrich Ohmann.

H5 Stadtpark U4 to Stadtpark

Old Vienna Walk

A walk round the historic Innere Stadt gives you the chance to see some of Vienna's best-known sights and linger in its coffeehouses.

DISTANCE: 3.5km (2.2 miles) **ALLOW:** 2 hours

START

BURGRING

E5 U3 to Volkstheater

❶ Start at the Burgtor on the Ringstrasse. Walk through this triumphal arch into the Heldenplatz. On your right is the Neue Hofburg, containing the National Library and two museums.

❷ Continue through the arches into the main courtyard ("In der Burg") of the Hofburg (▷ 26–27). Through the Schweizertor (Swiss Gate) on the south side, the Burgkapelle and the sacred and profane treasuries (Schatzkammer) are reached.

❸ From the main courtyard approach the Michaelertor and the entrance to the Imperial Apartments. Exiting onto Michaelerplatz, turn right for Josefsplatz.

❹ Head along Augustinerstrasse, passing the Augustinerkirche (▷ 32), then the Albertina (▷ 32), on your right. Behind the Staatsoper (▷ 35) you will see Hotel Sacher (▷ 112).

❺ Beyond it turn left into Kärntner Strasse, Vienna's premier shopping precinct. Turn right down Annagasse, for the baroque Annakirche (▷ 32).

❻ Then turn left into Seilerstätte and left again into Himmelpfortgasse. At Kärntner Strasse turn right and continue to Stephansplatz and St. Stephen's Cathedral (▷ 31). Opposite is the modern Haas-Haus (1990), by Hans Hollein.

❼ Walk west along the Graben past the Plague Column and the Peterskirche (▷ 35) down an alley on your right. Continue west along picturesque Naglergasse to the southwestern edge of Am Hof.

❽ Proceed along the Heidenschuss through the Freyung (▷ 25), and turn left through the Ferstel arcade. Emerging on Herrengasse, walk back (left) to the Hofburg's Michaelertor.

BURGRING

END

Shopping

ALTMANN & KÜHNE

www.altmann-kuehne.at

The maker of Vienna's best chocolates and the most creative candy.

F4 Graben 30 533 09 27 Mon–Fri 9–6.30, Sat 10–5 U1, U3 to Stephansplatz

ARCADIA OPERA SHOP

www.arcadia.at

The shop for serious opera buffs. Next to the Opera (▷ 35).

F5 Kärntner Strasse 40 513 95 68 Mon–Sat 9.30–7, Sun 10–7 U1, U2, U4 to Karlsplatz/Oper

AUGARTEN

www.augarten.at

Viennese Porcelain with floral designs produced at the factory in Augarten park (▷ 100).

F4 Spiegelgasse 3 512 14 94 Mon–Sat 10–6 U1, U3 to Stephansplatz

C. BEDNARCZYK

www.bednarczyk.at

Specialist in 18th-century pieces. Paintings, glass, porcelain, cabinets and jewelry and silver.

F4 Dorotheergasse 12 512 44 45 Mon–Fri 11–5, Sat 10–1 U1, U2, U4 to Karlsplatz/Oper

DERBY-HANDSCHUHE

www.derby-handschuhe-wien.at

Devoted entirely to gloves. The fact that this store remains in business may have something to do with Viennese winters.

F5 Plankengasse 5 512 57 03 Mon–Fri 10–6, Sat 10–5 U1, U3 to Stephansplatz

DOBLINGER

www.doblinger.at

Mecca for music-lovers and performers: sheet music, books, instruments and CDs.

F4 Dorotheergasse 10 515 03-0 Mon–Fri 9.30–6.30, Sat 10–1 U1, U3 to Stephansplatz

DOROTHEUM

www.dorotheum.com

An auction house founded in the early 18th century in an old convent. You can find everything from the worthless to the priceless, with some items marked for direct sale. They hold 600 auctions a year.

F5 Dorotheergasse 17 515 600 Art auctions: see website. Exhibitions of objects: Mon–Fri 10–6, Sat 9–5 U1, U2, U4 to Karlsplatz/Oper

BOOK TRADE

Austria imposes *Mehrwertsteuer* (Value Added Tax) on books, which makes foreign paperbacks very expensive. Expect prices at least 50 percent above what you'd pay for a book in your own home town, and even more for newspapers. Austria's own publishing industry suffers from the small size of the local market, and from the dominance of big German firms, ever ready to scoop up promising Austrian authors for their lists.

DUFT UND KULTUR

This shop has lovely smells from Africa and the Orient to sweeten any room of the house.

F4 Tuchlauben 17 532 39 60 Mon–Fri 10–6.30, Sat 10–5 U1, U3 to Stephansplatz

FREYTAG & BERNDT

www.freytagberndt.at

Travel bookshop stocking English titles, especially books on Central Europe. Unrivaled selection of maps and street plans.

F4 Wallnerstrasser 3 533 86 85 Mon–Fri 9.30–6.30, Sat 9.30–6 U3 to Herrengasse

FRICK AM GRABEN

A bookshop selling primarily literature, with a small English department. Paperbacks and children's books are strong points.

F4 Graben 27 533 9914-0 Mon–Fri 9–7, Sat 9.30–6 U1, U3 to Stephansplatz

FRICK IN DER KÄRNTNER STRASSE

www.buchhandlung-frick.at

The best shop for books on architecture and the decorative arts, with material on Viennese art and architecture.

F5 Kärntner Strasse 30 513 73 64 Mon–Fri

9–7, Sat 9.30–6 U1, U2, U4 to Karlsplatz/Oper or U1, U3 to Stephansplatz

GALERIE ERNST HILGER

www.hilger.at

Contemporary Austrian art. Eleven special exhibitions each year.

F4 Dorotheergasse 5 512 53 15 Tue–Fri 10–6 (Thu 10–8), Sat 10–4 U1, U3 to Stephansplatz

GALERIE HEIKE CURTZE

www.heikecurtze.com

This gallery sells work by some of Austria's leading modern artists.

G5 Seilerstätte 15 512 93 75 Tue–Fri 12–7, Sat 12–4 U1, U3 to Stephansplatz

GALERIE NÄCHST ST. STEPHAN

www.schwartzwaelder.at

Avant-garde art from Austria and abroad.

G4 Grünangergasse 1–2 512 12 66 Mon–Fri 11–6, Sat 11–4 U1, U3 to Stephansplatz

GALERIE NEBEHAY

www.nebehay.at

Christian Nebehay is a leading expert on Klimt and Schiele. His shop also sells old prints and antiquarian books, as well as his own books on his specialist field—early 20th-century art.

F5 Annagasse 18 512 18 01 Mon–Fri 9.30–1, 2–6 U1, U2, U4 to Karlsplatz/Oper

GALERIE WOLFRUM

The specialist shop for art books, with an excellent print department.

F5 Augustinerstrasse 10 512 53 980 Mon–Fri 10–6, Sat 10–5 U1, U2, U4 to Karlsplatz/Oper

GEA

Shoes in a laid-back style. Look for the Waldviertler ankle boot.

G5 Himmelpfortgasse 26 512 19 67 Mon–Fri 10–6, Sat 10–5 U1, U3 to Stephansplatz

HAAS & HAAS

www.haas-haas.at

A stylish gift shop that stocks teas and tea paraphernalia.

F5 Stephansplatz 4 512 97 70 Shop: Mon–Fri 9–6.30, Sat 9–6. Teahouse: Mon–Fri 8–8, Sat 8–6.30, Sun 9–6 U1, U3 to Stephansplatz

SACHERTORTE

The origin of Sachertorte, the chocolate cake for which the city is renowned, is so hotly disputed that there have been lawsuits between rival claimants. Those who want authenticity buy at Café Sacher (▷ 43; they will also mail). Hotel Imperial (▷ 112) also offers (to a different recipe) an Imperialtorte. Or you can buy a perfectly acceptable Sachertorte for much less at any branch of the Aida chain of cafés (▷ 43).

J. & L. LOBMEYR

www.lobmeyr.at

The famous glassware is still made to the 19th-century neo-baroque and neo-Renaissance design. Above the family-run shop is a small exhibition of J. & L. Lobmeyr's early work.

F5 Kärntner Strasse 26 512 05 08 Mon–Fri 10–7, Sat 10–6 U1, U3 to Stephansplatz

JULIUS MEINL AM GRABEN

www.meinlamgraben.at

A fine grocer with a superb delicatessen counter, a café, bars and an expensive restaurant (▷ 45), all with different hours from the shop.

F4 Graben 19 532 33 34 Mon–Fri 8–7.30, Sat 9–6 U1, U3 to Stephansplatz

KNIZE

www.knize.at

Exclusive men's tailors also notable for the 1913 facade and the interior designed by Adolf Loos.

F4 Graben 13 512 21 19 Mon–Fri 9.30–6, Sat 10–5 U1, U3 to Stephansplatz

KÖCHERT

www.koechert.at

Jewelers to the royal and imperial court since 1814, this reputable shop is elegant and restrained.

F5 Neuer Markt 15 512 58 28 Mon–Fri 10–6, Sat 10–5 U1, U3 to Stephansplatz

METZGER

Specializes in candles, as well as honey cakes, gingerbread, chocolates and other gift items.
F4 Stephansplatz 7
512 34 33 Mon–Fri 9–7, Sat 9–6 U1, U3 to Stephansplatz

MODELLE-HÜTE

www.hochhausherrengasse.at
Large range of traditional hats, in all shapes and colors, as well as scarves and amber jewelry.
E4 Herrengasse 6–8
Mon–Fri 10–7, Sat 10–6
U3 to Herrengasse

MÜHLBAUER

www.muehlbauer.at
This flagship shop sells the distinctive Mühlbauer hats favored by Brad Pitt and Madonna.
F4 Seilergasse 10
512 22 41 Mon–Fri 10–6.30, Sat 10–6 U1, U3 to Stephansplatz

ÖSTERREICHISCHE WERKSTÄTTEN

www.austrianarts.com
Glass ornaments and gifts, with Secessionist designs and attractive enamel.
F4 Kärntner Strasse 6 512 24 18 Mon–Fri 10–6.30, Sat 10–6 U1, U3 to Stephansplatz

OTTO FEILER

www.ottofeiler.at
Beautifully fashioned silver goods (new and antique)—including jewelry, cutlery, pill boxes and rosaries.
G4 Strobelgasse 1
513 29 40 Mon–Fri 10–6, Sat 10–5 U1, U3 to Stephansplatz

PINOCCHIO

A selection of children's gifts crafted from wood, including toys, clocks and picture frames.
F5 Augustinerstrasse 7
6991 954 7102 Daily 10–6 U1, U2, U4 to Karlsplatz/Oper Trams 1, 2, D to Opernring

ROBERT HORN

www.rhorns.com
A cult shop offering fine leather briefcases, handbags, wallets and more.
F4 Bräunerstrasse 7
513 82 94 Mon–Fri 10–6.30, Sat 10–5 U1, U3 to Stephansplatz

SCHÖNBICHLER

www.teagschwendner.com
The Viennese come here to buy English marmalade and tea, Scotch whisky and Christmas pudding.
G4 Wollzeile 4
512 18 16 Mon–Fri 9–6.30, Sat 9–5 U1, U3 to Stephansplatz

ANTIQUES SHOPS

While other shops are scattered around the whole district, antiques shops are concentrated in the side streets running from Graben to the Hofburg. In the Bräunerstrasse, Dorotheergasse and Spiegelgasse you will find an ever-changing display of what has survived from the collections of the Viennese art-loving middle class and nobility. The Dorotheum (▷ 38) holds auctions.

SHAKESPEARE & COMPANY

Large selection of books in English and Austrian and stacks of novels and history books.
F3 Sterngasse 2
535 5053 Mon–Sat 9–9 U1, U4 to Schwedenplatz

STEFFL

www.kaufhaus-steffl.at
Futuristic shop full of top labels. Also a floor devoted to cosmetics. Media café, bar and restaurant.
F5 Kärntner Strasse 19
930 56-0 Mon–Fri 10–8, Sat 9.30–6 U1, U3 to Stephansplatz

WIENER INTERIEUR

Specializes in smaller Jugendstil and art deco objects.
F4 Dorotheergasse 14
512 28 98 Mon–Fri 10–6, Sat 10–1 U1, U2, U4 to Karlsplatz/Oper

WOKA

www.woka.at
For something with the appearance of the Wiener Werkstätte, reproduction lamps from this high-quality workshop may be the answer. Great style.
G4 Singerstrasse 16
513 29 12 Mon–Fri 10–6, Sat 10–5 U1, U3 to Stephansplatz

Entertainment and Nightlife

BADESCHIFF WIEN

www.badeschiff.at

Forget the ocean cruise: Vienna has its very own ship pool in the Donaukanal downstream from Schwedenplatz. The boat is narrow but 30m (98ft) long, and has an outdoor pool that is open through the summer. Day or two-hour tickets available. The ship also holds the Holy-Moly! restaurant (▷ 45).

H3 Franz-Josefs-Kai between Schwedenplatz and Urania Pool: summer 8am–midnight U1, U4 to Schwedenplatz Trams 1, 2 to Schwedenplatz

DANZÓN

www.danzon.club

A colorful Latin dance bar with theme nights and dance classes.

F5 Johannesgasse 3 699 1234 61 52 Bar: daily 6.30pm–early hours; club: Thu–Sat 10pm–late U1, U2, U4 to Karlsplatz/Oper Trams 2, D to Kärntner Ring

EDEN BAR

www.edenbar.at

An elegant dress code and live music are characteristic of this exclusive bar in the shadow of St. Stephen's. To be a regular guest at the Eden Bar stamps you as a member of Vienna's high society.

F4 Liliengasse 2 512 74 50 Thu–Sat 10pm–4am U1, U3 to Stephansplatz

ETABLISSEMENT RONACHER

www.musicalvienna.at

This variety theater, with a late 19th-century interior, has reopened after a long period of darkness. Its schedule is unpredictable—from a spectacular à la André Heller to a Broadway musical. No shows on Wednesdays.

G5 Seilerstätte 9 588 85 Box office: Mon–Sat 10–1, 2–6, Sun 2–6 U1, U3 to Stephansplatz, U4 to Stadtpark

KAMMERSPIELE

www.josefstadt.org

This subsidiary stage of the Theater in der Josefstadt (▷ 61) puts on plays—often comedies and farces, and recycled London West End hits.

G4 Rotenturmstrasse 20 42 700-300 tickets with credit card U1, U4 to Schwedenplatz

NIGHT MUSIC

You can now hear most types of jazz regularly in Vienna. In summer there is a jazz festival held partly in the Staatsoper (▷ 35), and there is an open-air festival on the Donauinsel (Danube Island) in July. Performances generally start at 9pm but check the current *Wien Programm* (available at all Tourist Information Bureaux). The night scene has grown livelier and the Bermuda Dreieck (Bermuda Triangle, ▷ 13) is a magnet for gilded youth. There you will find idiosyncratic bars, trendy restaurants, discos, beer cellars, live music and cabaret.

KURSALON

www.kursalonwien.at

The Strauss summer festival takes place at the Kursalon in the Stadtpark (originally a place where bourgeois park visitors could take the spa water).

G5 Johannesgasse 33 512 57 90 U4 to Stadtpark Tram 2 to Weihburggasse

NIGHTFLY'S CLUB

www.nightflys.at

An intimate American cellar bar where you'll hear golden oldies, from Glenn Miller to Frank Sinatra. There are over 250 cocktail choices.

F4 Dorotheergasse 14 512 99 79 Summer daily 6pm–3am; winter 8pm–3am U1, U3 to Stephansplatz

ÖSTERREICHISCHES FILMMUSEUM

www.filmmuseum.at

The dedicated Austrian Film Museum has kept this shrine to the movies alive. It screens Austrian and other films, with the theme changing monthly.

F5 Augustinerstrasse 1 (Albertina) 533 70 54 Films: check website for show times. Bar: 10am–midnight U1, U2, U4 to Karlsplatz/Oper

PORGY & BESS

www.porgy.at

A club that showcases jazz musicians both from Austria and the rest of the world. Performances usually start at 8 or 8.30pm (check website).

G4 Riemergasse 11 512 88 11 Daily 5pm–late U3 to Stubentor

ROTER ENGEL

www.roterengel.at

This venue exemplifies the best of the Bermuda Dreieck (Bermuda Triangle) area. It calls itself a *Wein und Lieder-bar* (wine and song bar) and serves wine with cheeses. It also has rhythm and blues and folk evenings.

G3 Rabensteig 5 535 41 05 Daily 5pm–4am U1, U4 to Schwedenplatz Trams 1, 2 to Schwedenplatz

STAATSOPER

www.wiener-staatsoper.at

The Vienna State Opera (▷ 35) ranks among the world's top opera houses. Viennese music lovers can be merciless, and being director of the State Opera is reputedly the most brutal job in the country. Among those who have held the post are Gustav Mahler, Richard Strauss, Herbert von Karajan and Lorin Maazel. World War II bombs destroyed most of the interior. The ceremonial staircase and the foyers have been restored.

F5 Opernring 2 51444-2250; ticket info: 51444-2950 U1, U2, U4 to Karlsplatz/Oper Trams 1, 2, 71, D, Badner Bahn to Kärntner Ring/Oper

STADTFEST

www.stadtfest-wien.at

On a weekend in spring, the Inner City (Innere Stadt) hosts a variety of different kinds of events connected with the Vienna City Festival. Organized by the conservative People's Party, it is their answer to the Social Democrats' Festival on the Danube Island (Donauinsel).

F4 Inner City One weekend in spring U3 to Herrengasse

MUSICAL TRADITION

Music has been part of the city's culture from earliest times. In the mid-18th century Haydn and then Mozart began to displace the long-dominant Italian composers in public esteem. The 19th century was also rich in musical talent, some of it imported (Beethoven, Brahms) but much homegrown (Schubert, Bruckner, Hugo Wolf, Strauss father and son and Mahler). Later, Arnold Schönberg pioneered the 12-tone system, while his erstwhile pupils, such as Alban Berg and Anton von Webern, made the "Second Viennese School" world famous.

STRANDBAR HERRMANN

www.strandbarherrmann.at

Situated where the River Wien debouches into the Danube Canal, this beach club—Vienna's first—has deckchairs, dining and DJ music in the evening.

H3 Donaukanal-Promenade/Urania Apr–Sep daily 10am–2am U1, U4 to Schwedenplatz Trams 1, 2 to Julius-Raab-Platz

TEL-AVIV BEACH

www.neni.at

The beach, on the northern bank of the Danube Canal, on the edge of the old Jewish Quarter, has proved extremely popular since it opened in 2009. There are beach chairs in the sand, Mediterranean food with an Israeli slant and a program of films and other events. The service may be lackluster, but nobody seems to mind.

G2 Donaukanal at Herminengasse Apr–Oct daily noon–midnight U2, U4 to Schottenring

WIENER KAMMEROPER

www.theater-wien.at

A seedbed for talent for the Volksoper, Staatsoper or abroad. The schedule includes many lesser-known operas. A small, intimate space.

G4 Fleischmarkt 24 Tickets 58 885 U1, U4 to Schwedenplatz Trams 1, 2 to Schwedenplatz

Restaurants

PRICES

Prices are approximate, based on a 3-course meal for one person.

€€€ over €40

€€ €20–€40

€ under €20

AIDA (€)

www.aida.at

One of the cafés in the classic chain known for its devotion to the color pink—from the cakes to the staff uniforms.

F4 Singerstrasse 1 512 29 77 Mon–Fri 7am–10pm, Sat–Sun 8am–10pm U1, U3 to Stephansplatz. Also at: Bognergasse 3, Wollzeile 28, Rotenturmstrasse 24

AT EIGHT (€€€)

www.ateight-restaurant.com

Award-winning cuisine using seasonal produce. Each afternoon, staff convert the hotel breakfast room into a stylish restaurant space for dinner.

F6 Kärtner Ring 8 22 1 22 3830 Daily 6pm–11.30pm U1, U2, U4 to Karlsplatz/Oper Trams 1, 2, D to Opernring

BEIM CZAAK (€)

www.czaak.com

A traditional *Beisl* in a quiet corner. Viennese cuisine, but with the emphasis on its Czech origins.

G4 Postgasse 15 513 72 15 Mon–Sat 11–midnight U1, U4 to Schwedenplatz

BRISTOL LOUNGE (€€€)

www.bristolvienna.com

Many consider this elegant restaurant in the Hotel Bristol the best in town, with the finest Viennese cuisine. Set lunch menu for €24.

F5 Mahlerstrasse 2 515 16-553 Daily 7pm–11pm U1, U2, U4 to Karlsplatz/Oper

CAFÉ CENTRAL (€€)

www.palaisevents.at

Popular café and restaurant in the Palais Ferstel (▷ 25). Marble columns, vaulted ceilings and a reasonably priced lunch menu. There's a less formal patisserie at Herrengasse 7.

E4 Corner of Herrengasse and Strauchgasse 533 37 64-26 Mon–Sat 7.30am–10pm, Sun 10–10 U3 to Herrengasse

FOOD FROM AROUND THE WORLD

Although Vienna has had a large international community since the 1970s, the choice of non-Viennese cooking is not great. Pizza and pasta are ubiquitous, and the number of Chinese and Japanese restaurants is growing; yet there are surprisingly few French restaurants of repute, the Greek and Spanish selection is disappointing, and the cuisines of some other territories are virtually unknown. The list here reflects the choice available.

CAFÉ DIGLAS (€)

www.diglas.at

Founded in 1923, it was a comparative latecomer to the coffeehouse scene. Its most famous regular customer was Franz Lehár.

G4 Wollzeile 10 512 57 65 Daily 8am–10.30pm U1, U3 to Stephansplatz

CAFÉ PRÜCKEL (€€)

www.prueckel.at

Classic old-school Ringstrasse coffeehouse. The traditional Viennese cooking is a cut above the average, but most come here to soak up the vibe.

G4 Stubenring 24 512 61 15 Daily 8.30am–10pm U3 to Stubentor Tram 2 to Stubentor

CAFÉ SACHER (€€)

www.sacher.com

Elegant, traditional café in the famous hotel, and a place to get the renowned Sachertorte.

F5 Philharmonikerstrasse 4 51 456 0 Daily 8am–midnight U1, U2, U4 to Karlsplatz/Oper

LE CIEL (€€€)

www.leciel.at

Restaurant on the top floor of the Grand Hotel Wien (▷ 112) serving excellent fusion cooking that blends French and Austrian influences.

F5 Kärtner Ring 9 515 80 9100 U1, U2, U4 to Karlsplatz/Oper Trams 1, 2, D to Opernring

DEMEL (€€–€€€)

www.demel.at

Founded in 1786, the business was taken over by Christoph Demel in 1857 and remained in the family until Anna Demel's death in 1956. The staff are decked out in black uniforms with white frills. The lavish interior is a restoration dating from the 1930s.
F4 Kohlmarkt 14 535 17 17-0 Daily 9–7 U3 to Herrengasse Bus 2A to Michaelerplatz

DO & CO (€€€)

www.doco.com

The restaurant's superb location in Hans Hollein's Haas Haus offers a view of the cathedral from the best tables. The excellent cuisine includes Far and Middle East cooking mixed with local tradition. Also an excellent hotel (▷ 112).
F4 Stephansplatz 12 535 39 69 Daily 12–3, 6–midnight U1, U3 to Stephansplatz

ESTERHAZYKELLER (€)

www.esterhazykeller.at

The Esterhazys gave free wine to the populace here during the 1683 Turkish siege. The wine is no longer free but it's still very good value, as is the simple food.
F4 Haarhof 1 (off Wallnerstrasse) 533 34 82 Mon–Fri 11–11, Sat–Sun 4–11 U3 to Herrengasse

FABIOS (€€€)

www.fabios.at

When opened a few years back, Fabio Giacobello's designer restaurant became the most trendy of Vienna's top-level eateries almost overnight. The glass facade can be removed, weather permitting. Its creative cuisine has made it a celebrity hot spot.
F4 Tuchlauben 4–6 532 22 22 Mon–Sat 10–1 U1, U3 to Stephansplatz

FIGLMÜLLER (€€)

www.figlmuller.at

One of two family-run restaurants serving huge schnitzels. The restaurant on the Wollzeile serves wine, but not beer. The restaurant prides itself on its Wiener schnitzels.
G4 Wollzeile 5 512 61 77 Daily 11–10. Closed Aug U1, U3 to Stephansplatz
Also at: G4 Bäckerstrasse 6 512 17 60 Daily 12–11. Closed Jul U1, U3 to Stephansplatz

ALTERNATIVES

There are a growing number of possibilities for serious fish eaters, including the popular Nordsee chain. For the freshest and best, be prepared to dig deep in the pocket. The pizza trade expands even faster than hamburger joints in this part of the world, and there is now a good choice of places in central Vienna serving freshly made pizzas. There are even, in a city of mainly meat-eaters, a number of vegetarian restaurants.

HAAS & HAAS (€€)

www.haas-haas.at

An annex to the Haas & Haas Teahouse behind St. Stephen's Cathedral, this restaurant excels with a small but fine menu and good Austrian wines. It also has a delightful garden in the courtyard of the Teutonic Order.
G4 Stephansplatz 4 512 26 66 Mon–Sat 8–8, Sun 9–7 U1, U3 to Stephansplatz

HEINER (€€)

www.heiner.co.at

The branch overlooking Kärntner Strasse is excellent, but the little Biedermeier interior of Heiner in the Wollzeile is irresistible. The cakes and pastries are really superb and the coffee good; fine handmade chocolates, too. Special goodies for diabetics are available.
F5 Kärntner Strasse 21–3 512 68 63 Mon–Sat 8.30–7.30, Sun 10–7.30 U1, U3 to Stephansplatz
Also at: G4 Wollzeile 9 512 23 43 Mon–Sat 8.30–7, Sun and hols 10–7 U1, U3 to Stephansplatz

HOLLMANN SALON (€€)

www.hollmann-salon.at

Set in a square off the main street. Diners enjoy regional, organic Austrian food at long, shared tables. The fixed-price set menus at lunchtime are particularly good value.

G4 Im Heiligenkreuzerhof, Grashofgasse 3 96 119 6040 Mon–Fri 12–3, 6–10, Sat 10–3, 6–10 U1, U4 to Schwedenplatz Trams 1, 2 to Schwedenplatz

HOLY-MOLY! (€€)

www.badeschiff.at

Aboard the Badeschiff Wien (▷ 41), the Holy-Moly! serves excellent cuisine at reasonable prices. There's a bar on the top deck and a disco below.

H3 Franz-Josefs-Kai between Schwedenplatz and Urania 660 31 24 703 May to mid-Sep daily 10am–1am; mid-Sep to Apr 6pm–1am U1, U4 to Schwedenplatz Trams 1, 2 to Schwedenplatz

KERN'S BEISL (€€)

www.kernbeisl.at

A wonderful place to experience honest Austrian cooking and a wide selection of Austrian wines by the glass. Unpretentious restaurateurship at its best.

F4 Kleeblattgasse 4 (off Tuchlauben) 533 91 88 Mon–Fri 9am–11pm U1, U3 to Stephansplatz

KORNAT (€€–€€€)

www.kornat.at

This Croatian restaurant serves fish flown in fresh from the Dalmatian coast with wines from Hvar and Korcula.

G3 Marc-Aurel-Strasse 8 535 65 18 Mon–Sat 11.30–3, 6–12 U1, U4 to Schwedenplatz

MEINL AM GRABEN (€€€)

www.meinlamgraben.at

A discreet gourmet stop in the only remaining branch of quality grocer Meinl. The best of Austrian cooking in an informal atmosphere; fabulous wines.

F4 Graben 19 532 33 34-6000 Mon–Wed 8.30am–midnight, Thu–Fri 8am–midnight, Sat 9am–midnight U3, U1 to Stephansplatz

STREET EATS

The most popular quick bite is *würst* (sausage). Stands typically serve hot dogs, German-style sausages and a uniquely Austrian invention: *käsekrainer* (grilled pork stuffed with cheese). On ordering a sausage, you'll be asked "sweet *(süss)* or spicy *(scharf)*?," referring to the type of mustard. In recent years, Middle Eastern doner kebab outfits have sprung up, offering satisfying sandwiches of spicy lamb, veal or chicken. Some of the best are at Restaurant Lale (▷ above).

PLACHUTTA (€€€)

www.plachutta.at

One of several Plachutta restaurants, the real draw at the Wollzeile branch is the *tafelspitz* (boiled beef), served in its own broth.

G4 Wollzeile 38 512 15 77 Daily 11am–midnight U3 to Stubentor Tram 2 to Stubentor

RESTAURANT LALE (€€)

www.lale.at

Located near to Schwedenplatz, this popular Turkish–Middle Eastern restaurant specializes in oversized kebabs and grilled meats, big pieces of fresh pita bread and satisfying sides like tzatziki and hummus. There's takeout if you're in a hurry.

G4 Franz-Josefs-Kai 29 535 27 36 Daily 11.30am–midnight U1, U4 to Schwedenplatz

WRENKH (€€)

www.wiener-kochsalon.com

Exquisite vegetarian cuisine with choices such as wild rice risotto with mushrooms, and Greek fried rice with vegetables, sheep's cheese and olives.

F4 Bauernmarkt 10 533 15 26 Mon–Sat 12–10 U1, U3 to Stephansplatz

Chefkonditor
Pfliegler

Largely undamaged by World War II, the Ringstrasse is one of Europe's great boulevards. It has many magnificent buildings created for cultural and political institutions, as well as elegant parks.

JOSEFSTADT
8
Schön-Bornpark
Piaristenkeller
Piaristenkirche
Maria-Treu-Kloster
Theater in der Josefstadt
Jugendgerichtshof
Arbeits- und Sozialgericht
Rathaus
Kabarett Niedermair
Vienna's English Theatre
Palais Auersperg
Weghuber-Park
Karl-Farkas-Park
St Ulrich
Ateliertheater
Kosmos Theater
Renaissance Theater
St Laurenz
Neubaugasse
Maria-Hilf-Kloster
Bundesländerplatz
Hofmobiliendepot
Haus des Meeres
Esterhazy-Park
Fritz-Grünbaum-Platz
Loquaiplatz
TAG
Florianigasse
Lange Gasse
Lammgasse
Schlösselgasse
Wickenburggasse
Tulpengasse
Lenaugasse
Piaristengasse
Josefstädter Strasse
Josefsgasse
Trautsongasse
AUERSPERGSTRASSE
Pfeilgasse
Lerchengasse
Strozzigasse
Zeltgasse
Neudeggergasse
LERCHENFELDER STRASSE
NEUSTIFTGASSE
Zieglergasse
Myrthengasse
BURGGASSE
Stuckgasse
Sigmundgasse
Stiftgasse
Spittelberggasse
Gutenberggasse
Kirchberggasse
Kandlgasse
Bandgasse
Hermanngasse
Westbahnstrasse
Siebensterngasse
Kirchengasse
Mondscheingasse
Zollergasse
Lindengasse
Seidengasse
Stollgasse
Richtergasse
Andreasgasse
Barnabitengasse
Schadekgasse
Amerlingstrasse
Otto-Bauergasse
Esterhazygasse
Schmalzhofgasse
Königseggasse
GUMPENDORFER STRASSE
HOFMÜHLGASSE
Corneliusgasse
Kaunitzgasse
Dürergasse
Luftbadgasse
LINKE WIENZEILE
Falcostiege
0
250 m
250 yds
3
4
5
6
7
B
C
D

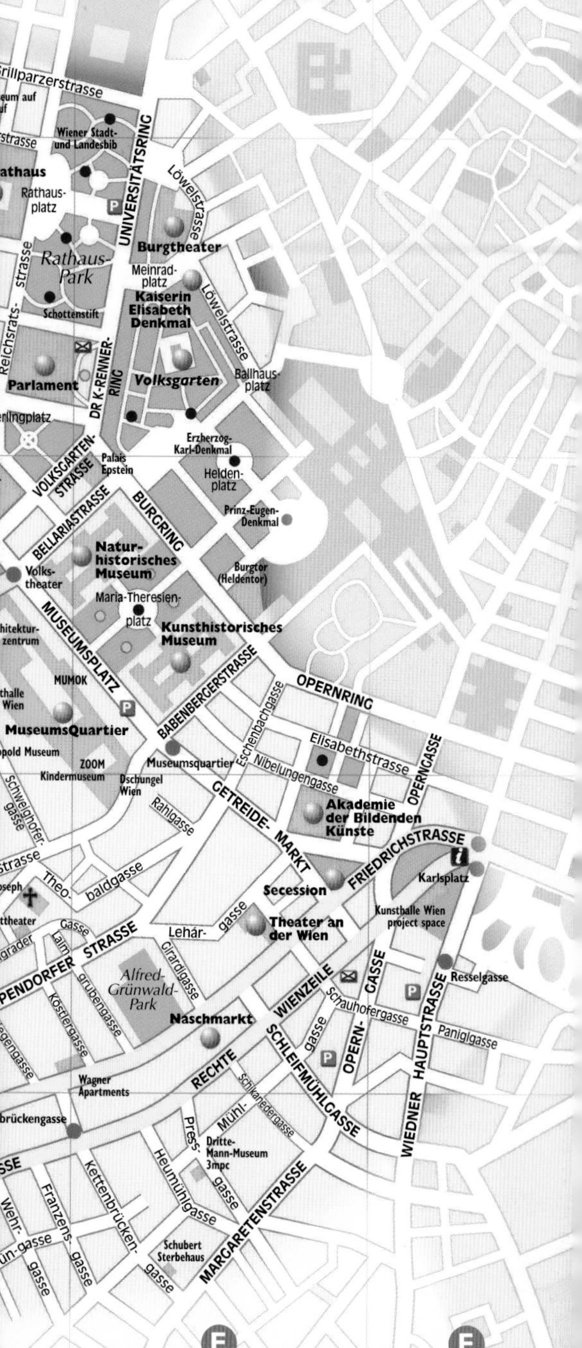

Grillparzerstrasse
Wiener Stadt- und Landesbib
Rathaus
Rathausplatz
UNIVERSITÄTSRING
Löwelstrasse
Burgtheater
Rathaus-Park
Meinradplatz
Kaiserin Elisabeth Denkmal
Schottenstift
Reichsrats-strasse
DR K.-RENNER-RING
Parlament
Volksgarten
Ballhausplatz
Erzherzog-Karl-Denkmal
VOLKSGARTEN-STRASSE
Palais Epstein
Heldenplatz
BELLARIASTRASSE
BURGRING
Prinz-Eugen-Denkmal
Naturhistorisches Museum
Volkstheater
Burgtor (Heldentor)
Maria-Theresien-platz
MUSEUMSPLATZ
Kunsthistorisches Museum
MUMOK
BABENBERGERSTRASSE
Eschenbachgasse
OPERNRING
MuseumsQuartier
ZOOM Kindermuseum
Museumsquartier
Elisabethstrasse
Nibelungengasse
OPERNGASSE
Dschungel Wien
Rahlgasse
GETREIDE-MARKT
Akademie der Bildenden Künste
FRIEDRICHSTRASSE
Karlsplatz
Theobaldgasse
Secession
Lehárgasse
Theater an der Wien
Kunsthalle Wien project space
Laimgrubengasse
STRASSE
Girardigasse
WIENZEILE
Resselgasse
Alfred-Grünwald-Park
Köstlergasse
Schleifmühlgasse
Schauhofergasse
Paniglgasse
Naschmarkt
OPERN-GASSE
WIEDNER HAUPTSTRASSE
RECHTE
SCHLEIFMÜHLGASSE
Wagner Apartments
Schikanedergasse
Mühlgasse
Pressgasse
Dritte-Mann-Museum 3mpc
Heumühlgasse
Kettenbrückengasse
Franzensgasse
MARGARETENSTRASSE
Wehrgasse
Schubert Sterbehaus
E
F

Akademie der Bildenden Künste

Otto Wagner's former apartment (left); statue of Schiller (middle) outside the Academy of Fine Arts (right)

THE BASICS

www.akbild.ac.at

E6

Schillerplatz 3

58 816-2222

Tue–Sun 10–6. Closed 1 Jan, 24–25 Dec, 31 Dec

U1, U2, U4 to Karlsplatz/Oper

Trams 1, 2 to Babenberger Strasse

Call in advance for access at Makartgasse entrance

Moderate

Audio guide

HIGHLIGHTS

- *Last Judgment*, Hieronymus Bosch
- *Views of Venice*, Antonio Guardi
- *Family in a Courtyard*, Pieter de Hooch
- Sketches for Banqueting House, Whitehall, Rubens

In 1907, Adolf Hitler was denied entry to the Academy of Fine Arts for his poor rendering of human heads. He tried a second time and was rejected by the academy's architecture professor, Otto Wagner, because he lacked the requisite academic qualifications.

The building The academy was completed in 1876 by one of the greatest architects of the Ringstrassen era, Theophil Hansen, whose other work includes the classical Parliament, the Stock Exchange and numerous neo-Renaissance palaces. In the middle of the square in front is a statue of the poet Friedrich Schiller (1759–1805). Along the facade are figures from antiquity associated with the fine arts; on the back are allegorical frescoes by August Eisenmenger, the academy's Professor for Painting in the late 19th century. Founded in 1692 by the painter Peter von Strudel, the academy numbers among its alumni the painter Friedensreich Hundertwasser, whose spectacular multihued house at Löwengasse, 3rd District, is a tourist attraction, and Fritz Wotruba, designer of the 1976 Wotruba Kirche (▷ 101), an extraordinary concrete structure.

The interior Anselm Feuerbach's ceiling fresco, *Downfall of Titans*, dominates the Basilical Hall; the collection of Dutch Masters is renowned and the graphic art collection is superb. Few teaching academies possess such a large graphic collection developed over 300 years.

Bust of Schiller (left) on the Burgtheater (right)

TOP 25

Burgtheater

The Burgtheater is one of the oldest in the world and Austria's national theater in all but name. It is regarded as one of the best German-language theaters.

Origins The name is taken from the court theater that stood on the edge of the Hofburg (on Michaelerplatz) from the time of Maria Theresa (1741) until 1888.

Architecture This neo-Renaissance building by Karl von Hasenauer and Gottfried Semper opened in 1888, but it was soon altered; so much attention in the design had been paid to architectural proportion and so little to function that some of the boxes faced away from the stage and the acoustics were appalling. An anecdote claimed that "In the Parliament you can't hear anything, in the Rathaus you can't see anything and in the Burgtheater you can neither see nor hear anything."

Decorative plan Inside and out, the Burgtheater is a symbolic celebration of the history of drama. On the central facade are monuments to the world's greatest playwrights. The ceremonial stairways that rise through the two wings toward the auditorium hold busts of the great Austrian and German dramatists. Gustav Klimt, his brother Ernst and Franz von Matsch decorated the ceilings above the stairway with frescoes depicting the history of theater. Oil portraits of famous Viennese actors and actresses hang in the foyer.

THE BASICS

www.burgtheater.at

E4

Universitätsring 2

51444-4140

Backstage theater tours: daily at 3pm. Closed 24 Dec, Good Friday, Jul and Aug except for tours. No tours during afternoon performances

U2 to Schottentor

Trams 1, D to Burgtheater

Good; by prior arrangement

Moderate

HIGHLIGHTS

Exterior

- View from the Rathaus across Ringstrasse

Interior

- *Thespiscart*, Gustav Klimt
- *Globe Theatre, London*, Gustav Klimt
- *Theater at Taormina*, Gustav Klimt
- *Medieval Mystery Theater*, Ernst Klimt
- *Molière's Le Malade Imaginaire*, Ernst Klimt

Kunsthistorisches Museum

TOP 25

HIGHLIGHTS

- *The Tower of Babel*, Brueghel
- *Madonna in the Meadow*, Raphael
- *Infanta Margareta Teresa*, Velázquez
- *Gold Salt Cellar*, Cellini

TIP

- Note Antonio Canova's dramatic *Theseus and the Centaur* on the grand staircase.

In the Museum of Art History you'll find the Habsburgs' fabulous collection, acquired over centuries by archdukes and emperors.

Origins The German architect Gottfried Semper planned to continue the sweep of the Neue Hofburg and build a parallel wing on the other side of the Heldenplatz; both wings were to extend across the Ringstrasse, creating a gigantic Imperial Forum of museums. The Museum of Art History and Natural History Museum (▷ 58) facing it are the partial realization of this attempt to bring together the widely dispersed Habsburg treasures. The Museum of Art History contains collections of paintings, Egyptian objects, sculpture, decorative art, coins and medals.

Clockwise from far left: Statue at the entrance of the Museum of Art History; portrait of Ferdinand II; the monument to Maria Theresa stands in the middle of the park; gallery of paintings; a bust on display in the museum

Architectural decoration Both the Museum of Art History and the Natural History Museum opposite are principally the work of Gottfried Semper; their interiors are by Karl Hasenauer. Between the museums lies a park, dominated by a monument to Maria Theresa (1740–80). Inside the Museum of Art History, marble and stucco are interspersed with murals; most notable is the ceiling fresco above the main landing, Mihály Munkácsy's *Apotheosis of Art*. The dome has medallions of collector-emperors. Hasenauer planned showrooms appropriate to their contents: the Egyptian collection, for example, is ornamented with columns from Luxor, a present from the Khedive to the Emperor Franz Josef. Benvenuto Cellini's Saliera (*Salt Cellar*), completed in 1543, is a gem of Renaissance craftsmanship.

THE BASICS

www.khm.at

E5

Maria-Theresien-Platz

525 24-0

Tue–Sun 10–6 (Thu until 9). Closed 24 Dec, shorter hours 1 Jan

Café in Cupola Hall

U2 to Museums-Quartier, U3 to Volkstheater

Trams 1, 2, D to Burgring

Good. Use the side entrance

Expensive. Combined ticket with the Imperial Treasury (▷ 26–27)

Frequent lectures and special exhibitions

MuseumsQuartier

TOP 25

Relaxing in the MuseumsQuartier (left); Museum of Modern Art (right)

THE BASICS

www.mqw.at
D5
Museumsplatz 1
523 58 81-1731
Daily 10–6 (some museums 10–7), Thu until 9
U2 to MuseumsQuartier, U2, U3 to Volkstheater
Good
Expensive (separate tickets); combined tickets available
Information point, ticket office and shop at entrance

HIGHLIGHTS

- *Death and Life*, Gustav Klimt
- Self-portrait by Egon Schiele (both in the Leopold Museum)

TIP

- Enjoy excellent traditional Viennese fare at Glacis Beisl, with an open-air terrace and trendy modern dining room. It is reached up two flights of steps at the rear of Museumplatz (526 56 60 Daily 11am–2am, kitchen until 11pm).

Museums in this quarter occupying the former Imperial Stables include the Kunsthalle and the Museum of Modern Art (MUseum MOderner Kunst or MUMOK). The Leopold Museum has fine works by Gustav Klimt, Egon Schiele and other artists of the period.

Meeting place Originally a futuristic "Book Tower" was planned to attract passersby and give the area a distinctive modern counterpoint to the architecture of the former Imperial Stables. But the grandiose concept here ended in compromise: only two museums exceed the height of the baroque stables in front of them. It is one of the liveliest places in the city, as it's central and easy to access. Young people meet here to see the cutting-edge exhibitions in the Kunsthalle at its heart or simply relax on the "*Enzis*" in the main courtyard—modernistic pieces of outdoor furniture on which you can lie, lean or sit.

The Leopold Museum Numerous cultural institutions, such as the Architekturzentrum, the Tanzquartier, the Children's Museum and the Museum of Modern Art, attract all kinds of visitors (some of them visit the MUMOK just for the fine view from its top floor). The flagship is definitely the Leopold Museum, with its excellent collection of Austrian fin-de-siècle art brought together by the collector (and ophthalmologist) Rudolf Leopold (1925–2010) and donated to the nation.

A summer concert (left) in the courtyard of the Rathaus (right)

TOP 25

Rathaus

The "new" City Hall (Neues Rathaus), built between 1872 and 1883 by architect Friedrich Schmidt, is possibly the finest neo-Gothic building in Vienna.

Inspiration The great buildings along the Ringstrasse, built between the 1860s and 1880s, exemplify the values of Liberalism—industrial modernization, democracy and capitalist enterprise. It is typically Viennese that this vision of the future was expressed in historic symbols. Schmidt chose as his model town halls typical of medieval Flanders. The main inspiration was the Brussels City Hall.

Inside and out The huge facade, with its traceried arches over the arcades, faces the Ringstrasse; above the arches are loggias and imposing balustrades adorned with statues. Rising from the middle is the 98m (321ft) tower topped by a 3.4m (11ft) copper statue. Inside, the grand staircases, noble promenades and richly decorated halls are a spectacle; don't miss the City Council Chamber and the Ceremonial Hall.

City Council The members of City Hall have a surprising degree of authority. While many smaller decisions are made on the district or neighborhood level (Vienna is divided into 23 separate districts), City Hall controls the budgets for schools, maintenance and parks, among other important items. It also reserves the right to veto decisions taken at local level.

THE BASICS

www.wien.gv.at/english/cityhall/tours.htm

D4

Friedrich-Schmidt-Platz 1

525 50

Tours: Mon, Wed, Fri 1pm. Closed session days, Good Fri, 24, 31 Dec

Rathauskeller (▷ 63)

U2 to Rathaus

Trams 1, 2, D to Rathausplatz

Good; phone or write in advance

Free

Visits by tour only, in German (apply at Stadtinformationszentrum in Schmidthalle). Audio guide in English

HIGHLIGHTS

- Statues
- Monument to President Karl Renner
- Opera films in summer; Christmas Market
- The Arkadenhof (arcaded courtyard)

Secession

TOP 25

The Secession's dome of gilded laurel leaves (left); detail of the facade (right)

THE BASICS

www.secession.at
E6
Friedrichstrasse 12
587 53 07
Tue–Sun 10–6. Closed 1 May, 1 Nov, 25 Dec
Outside summer café
U1, U2, U4 to Karlsplatz
Few
Moderate
Guided tours in English Sat 11am

HIGHLIGHTS

- Three carved gorgons over the doorway
- Inscription *Ver Sacrum* (Sacred Spring)
- Dome of gilded laurel leaves
- Picturesque sculpted owls
- Vast flower tubs on tortoise stands
- Statue: *Mark Antony in a Chariot Drawn by Lions* (1900), Arthur Strasser
- *Beethoven Frieze* (1902), Gustav Klimt

In a gesture of defiance toward the art establishment, this exhibition building of revolutionary design was built behind the Academy of Fine Arts. Its motto is inscribed over the entrance: "To every age its art, to art its freedom."

Vienna Secession In 1897, frustrated with the increasing conservatism of academic painting in Vienna and its stranglehold on the art market, a group of young artists broke away to form the subsequently famous "Vienna Secession." Its elected head was Gustav Klimt, whose *Beethoven Frieze*—an allegorical interpretation of the themes of the Ninth Symphony and a homage to the composer—can be seen here.

Jugendstil Klimt began his career working in the conventional genre of historical painting (exemplified by his work for the Burgtheater, ▷ 51). The Secession's style was associated with Jugendstil, the German version of art nouveau. It is sensuous and decorative, and achieves its best effects in architecture and stained glass.

The exhibition hall The breakaway artists needed a hall to exhibit their own works and to display avant-garde art from abroad. In 1898, Joseph Maria Olbrich completed the cube-like, towered and windowless Secession Building with a glass roof that provided daylight. The Viennese dubbed it the "Golden Cabbage" because of its gilded dome of entwined laurel leaves.

More to See

HAUS DES MEERES

www.haus-des-meeres.at

The "Flakturm" in Esterhazypark, one of six World War II antiaircraft towers, now houses crocodiles, snakes and spiders, as well as an aquarium. Views from the tower's outlook platform are impressive. The Museum of Torture (daily 10–6) is near by.

D6 Fritz-Grünbaum-Platz 1 (in Esterhazypark) 587 14 17 Daily 9–6 (Thu until 9). Shark feeding: Mon 10.30am, Wed 3pm Café U3 to Neubaugasse Buses 13A to Esterhazygasse/Haus des Meeres, 14A, 57A to Haus des Meeres Good Expensive

HOFMOBILIENDEPOT

www.hofmobiliendepot.at

A collection of furniture made by craftsmen for their Habsburg patrons from the time of Maria Theresa onward.

C6 Andreasgasse 7 524 33 57 Tue–Sun 10–6 U3 to Zieglergasse Good (use entrance on Andreasgasse) Moderate

KAISERIN ELISABETH DENKMAL

This monument was erected in the Volksgarten following the assassination of the popular empress by an anarchist in Geneva in 1898.

E4 Volksgarten (Burgtheater end) Trams 1, 2 to Burgtheater

NASCHMARKT

The Naschmarkt's two aisles are divided between restaurants and market stalls, selling everything from spices to fish. The two ends of the market are marked by buildings of the Viennese Jugendstil: at Getreidemarkt to the east is the Secession building (▷ 56) by Joseph Olbrich; and at Kettenbrückengasse to the west are two apartment buildings with floral ornaments by Otto Wagner, who also designed the nearby underground station of the U4.

E6 Wienzeile from Getreidemarkt to Kettenbrückengasse Mon–Fri 6am–7.30pm, Sat 6–5 U4 to Kettenbrückengasse

Picasso Triggerfish in Haus des Meeres

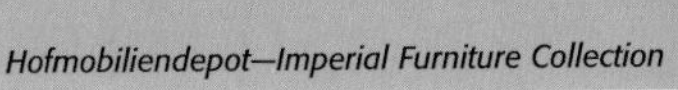

Hofmobiliendepot—Imperial Furniture Collection

NATURHISTORISCHES MUSEUM

www.nhm-wien.ac.at

Exhibits here include dinosaur skeletons and the 25,000-year-old Venus of Willendorf statuette.

E5 Maria-Theresien-Platz 521 77-0 Wed–Mon 9–6.30 (Wed until 9). Closed 1 Jan, 1 May, 1 Nov, 25 Dec U2 Volkstheater Trams 1, 2, D to Burgring Good; use entrance at Burgring 7 Moderate

PARLAMENT

www.parlament.gv.at

Visit the impressive marble hall and former Imperial Diet. The 1884 Historicist building was once the parliament of the western half of the Austro-Hungarian Empire. It was damaged by bombing during World War II; those areas accessible to the public were faithfully restored.

D4 Dr-Karl-Renner-Ring 3 40 110-2400 Guided tours: mid-Sep to mid-Jul Mon–Thu 11, 2, 3, 4, Fri 11, 1, 2, 3, 4, Sat 11–4 hourly; mid-Jul to mid-Sep Mon–Sat 11–4 hourly (except 15 Aug). No tours when Parliament is sitting. Closed public hols U2, U3 to Volkstheater Trams 1, 2, D to Parlament Good Inexpensive; tickets at adjacent shop

THEATER AN DER WIEN

www.theater-wien.at

Original owner Emanuel Schikaneder, librettist for Mozart's *Magic Flute*, complained that he had written "such a good piece, but Mozart ruined it all with his music." A shrewd impresario, Schikaneder would have appreciated the theater's success with such musicals as *Cats*, which ran for 11 years.

E6 Linke Wienzeile 6 588 85 Closed in summer U1, U2, U4 to Karlsplatz

VOLKSGARTEN

Dominated by the Doric Theseus-Tempel, the Volksgarten is an oasis of tranquility in the heart of the city.

E4 Dr-Karl-Renner-Ring Daily May–Sep 6am–10pm; Oct–Apr 6am–9pm U3 to Volkstheater Trams 1, 2, D to Parlament

Volksgarten

Relaxing with a book in the Volksgarten

Ringstrasse Circle

A walk along Vienna's Ringstrasse, which encircles the historic old city, offers a panorama of Historicist buildings and elegant parks.

DISTANCE: 5km (3 miles) **ALLOW:** 3 hours

START

SCHWEDENPLATZ

G3/4 U1, U4 to Schwedenplatz

❶ Walk along the Franz-Josefs-Kai westward from Schwedenplatz, then follow the Ring southward. On your right (in Deutschmeisterplatz) is the Rossauer Kaserne (once a barracks).

❷ Almost immediately to your left is Theophil Hansen's graceful Börse (Stock Exchange). Continue across Schottentor. Set back on your right you will pass the Votivkirche (▷ 71), then the neo-Renaissance university.

❸ Continue to the Burgtheater (▷ 51) opposite the Rathaus (City Hall, ▷ 55). Walk on past the Parlament (▷ 58) on your right, while to your left is the Volksgarten (▷ 58).

❹ Continuing east on the Ring you reach on your right the Naturhistorisches Museum (▷ 58), the Kunsthistorisches Museum (▷ 52–53) and the monument to Maria Theresa.

❺ Continue past Schillerplatz, with its statue to the poet Schiller in front of the Academy of Fine Arts, to the State Opera on your left (▷ 35).

❻ Continuing southeast on the Ring, you will see on your right the Hotel Imperial, then Schwarzenbergplatz. Next enter the Stadtpark (▷ 35) near the Strauss Monument (▷ 35).

❼ Leave the Stadtpark at the east end near the Museum of Applied Art. Cross the Ringstrasse to Georg-Coch-Platz and walk past Otto Wagner's Austrian Post Office Savings Bank (▷ 34).

❽ Finally you pass the former War Ministry, and follow the Ring round to its end, leaving the Urania cultural center on your right and returning to Schwedenplatz on Franz-Josefs-Kai.

SCHWEDENPLATZ

END

Shopping

CHRISTKINDLMARKT

www.christkindlmarkt.at

The biggest of Vienna's Christmas markets, which runs from mid-November until Christmas Eve. Goods include wooden crafts, sweets, leatherware and much more.

D4/E4 Rathausplatz Mid-Nov to 24 Dec Sun–Thu 10–9.30, Fri–Sat 10–10 (24 Dec 10–6) U2 to Rathaus Trams 1, D to Rathausplatz

HINTERMAYER BÜCHERMARKT

www.hintermayer.at

Lots of bargains at this bookshop with some English titles.

C6 Neubaugasse 29 and 36 523 02 25-13 Mon–Fri 10–6, Sat 10–4 U3 to Neubaugasse

INA KENT WIEN

www.inakent.com

Beautiful leather handbags and belts, with the maker's studio within the shop.

C6 Neubaugasse 34 699 1954 1090 Mon–Fri 11–7, Sat 11–6 U3 to Neubaugasse

NASCHMARKT

Vienna's gourmet market is a must to visit—sample its wares in the many small restaurants. A flea market is held next to it every Saturday from 6.30am to 6pm.

E6 Between the Linke and Rechte Wienzeile Permanent market Mon–Fri 6am–7.30pm, Sat 6–5. Restaurants to 10pm U4 to Kettenbrückengasse

NEUBAUGASSE

This fashionable side street in Vienna's 7th District offers an eclectic mix of shops with high-end fashion, secondhand clothing, books, music and cafés.

C6 Neubaugasse Most shops: Mon–Fri 9–7, Sat 10–6 U3 to Neubaugasse Bus 13A to Siebensterngasse; tram 46 to Strozzigasse

RAUMINHALT

www.rauminhalt.at

An unusual shop devoted to decorative objects and furniture of the last five decades. Plastic is particularly well represented, with the 1950s a specialty.

E6/E7 Schleifmühlgasse 13 650 409 9892 Tue–Fri 12–7, Sat 10–3 Bus 59A to Schleifmühlgasse; tram 62 to Paulanergasse

FINE CHINA

Since before the 18th century Vienna has produced a large quantity of objets d'art. The Secession (▷ 56), founded in 1897, was followed by the Wiener Werkstätte—its applied-art branch—and this gave renewed impetus to the creation of beautiful and functional items. The porcelain industry had its origins in Habsburg patronage of craft industries in the 18th century. The glassware from Lobmeyr is the product of the 19th-century Historicism Movement, which fostered imitations of Renaissance and baroque models.

RINGSTRASSEN-GALERIEN

www.ringstrassen-galerien.at

State-of-the-art shopping mall selling designer brands and gastronomic delicacies, from Asayake Sushi to Testa Rossa Coffee Bar.

F5 Kärntner Ring Shops: Mon–Fri 10–7, Sat 10–6; restaurants: daily 8am–1am U1, U2, U4 to Karlsplatz Trams 1, 2, D to Kärntner Ring/Oper

SPITTELBERG MARKET

All through the year local handicrafts are sold in the Spittelberg area in small shops, but before Christmas there is a street market.

D5 Spittelberggasse Mid-Nov to 23 Dec Mon–Fri 2pm–9pm, Sat–Sun 10–9 U3 to Neubaugasse Tram 49 to Stiftgasse

SZÁSZI HÜTE

www.szaszi.com

A traditional hatmaker—one of a dying breed of shops. The service is attentive.

E6 Mariahilferstrasse 4 522 56 52 Mon–Wed 10–6, Thu–Fri 10–12.30 U2 to MuseumsQuartier

Entertainment and Nightlife

BURGKINO

www.burgkino.at

This small foreign-language cinema keeps its finger on the pulse.

✚ E5 ✉ Opernring 19 ☎ 587 84 06 Ⓤ U1, U2, U4 to Karlsplatz/Oper

BURGTHEATER

If you speak German, try to watch a performance here. Otherwise, join a theater tour to see the superb frescoes by Gustav and Ernst Klimt above the stairway (▷ 51).

✚ E4 ✉ Universitätsring 2 ☎ 51 444 🚋 Trams 1, D to Burgtheater

CAMERA CLUB

www.camera-club.at

Old-school 1970s rock and music club which still draws leading national and international club bands. The best nights are Fridays and Saturdays. The rest of the week brings mainly DJs and dancing. Doors open at 11pm and the party goes on till the morning.

✚ C6 ✉ Neubaugasse 2 ☎ 523 30 63 Ⓤ U3 to Neubaugasse

FLEX

www.flex.at

One of downtown Vienna's best places for DJ music and live concerts, and still exuding alternative flair.

✚ F2 ✉ At the Danube Canal, downstairs from Augartenbrücke ☎ 533 75 25 ⏲ Daily 9pm–4am Ⓤ U2, U4 to Schottenring

PAVILLON IM VOLKSGARTEN

www.volksgarten-pavillon.at

A café by day and a disco with an open-air dance floor by night.

✚ E4 ✉ Burgring 1 ☎ 532 09 07 ⏲ Apr to mid-Sep daily 11am–2am Ⓤ U3 to Volkstheater 🚋 Trams 1, 2, D to Dr-Karl-Renner-Ring

THEATER AN DER WIEN—DAS NEUE OPERNHAUS

www.theater-wien.at

This theater (▷ 58), where Beethoven's *Fidelio* and Strauss's *Die Fledermaus* were first performed, now houses Vienna's "New Opera House," staging lesser-known and modern operas and ballets. Artistic standards are high. It also hosts classical concerts.

✚ E6 ✉ Linke Wienzeile 6 ☎ 588 30-200 Ⓤ U1, U2, U4 to Karlsplatz (Secession exit)

OUTRAGE AND EXCELLENCE

From 1986 until 1999, the Burgtheater was under the direction of Claus Peymann, a German whose radical productions and prejudiced political statements were hostile to the Austrian establishment. Resignations ensued when he imported 80 German actors, and although his contract was renewed, his application for Austrian citizenship was turned down. He was known for his challenging and imaginative productions of contemporary drama and the classics, and for nurturing the talent of Thomas Bernhard, Austria's greatest contemporary writer. In 2014 Karin Bergmann became the first woman to hold the position of director.

THEATER IN DER JOSEFSTADT

www.josefstadt.org

Close to Viennese hearts, this theater was once the powerhouse of the player-director Max Reinhardt. It was built in 1788 and renovated by Joseph Kornhäusel in neoclassical style in the 1820s. Outside, plaques honor Reinhardt and the 20th-century dramatist and librettist, Hugo von Hofmannsthal. Jugendstil drama is still played and promoted here.

✚ C4 ✉ Josefstädterstrasse 26 ☎ 42 700 300 Ⓤ U2 to Rathaus 🚋 Trams 2, 46 to Lederergasse/Strozzigasse

VIENNA'S ENGLISH THEATRE

www.englishtheatre.at

This theater, founded in 1963, presents solid productions of mainstream English-language drama and comedy, given a pep by a host of visiting stars.

✚ D4 ✉ Josefsgasse 12 ☎ 402 12 60-0 Ⓤ U2 to Rathaus, U3 to Volkstheater 🚋 Trams 1, D to Parlament

Restaurants

PRICES

Prices are approximate, based on a 3-course meal for one person.
€€€ over €40
€€ €20–€40
€ under €20

AKAKIKO (€€)

www.akakiko.at
Better value than many Japanese restaurants. The bonus here is the delightful roof terrace. There is a second outlet at Singerstrasse 4.
D6 Mariahilferstrasse 42–48 (5th floor of Gerngross store) 057 333 150 Daily 11–11 U3 to Neubaugasse

CAFÉ DRECHSLER (€)

www.cafedrechsler.at
The original Naschmarkt café with conveniently long opening hours. Plain furnishings and a good atmosphere.
E6 Linke Wienzeile 22 581 2044 Sun–Thu 8am–midnight, Fri–Sat 8am–2am U4 to Kettenbrückengasse

CAFÉ EILES (€)

Situated in a mainly residential area, this is a congenial, old-fashioned Viennese coffeehouse with window seats and niches. Small menu at midday.
D4 Josefstädterstrasse 2 405 3410 Mon–Fri 7am–10pm, Sat–Sun, hols 8am–10pm U2 to Rathaus Trams 1, D to Rathaus

CAFÉ LANDTMANN (€€)

www.landtmann.at
One of the classic Ringstrassen cafés, frequented by foreign correspondents reading international newspapers and by local ones attending the frequent press conferences held on its premises. Right next to the Burgtheater.
E4 Universitätsring 4 24 100100 Daily 7.30am–midnight. Live piano music Sun–Tue 8pm–11pm; Jul, Aug not Sun Trams 1, D to Burgtheater

CAFÉ SCHWARZENBERG (€€)

www.cafe-schwarzenberg.at
This is the oldest of the elegant Ringstrassen cafés, opened in 1861 when the boulevard was still under construction. There is a choice of newspapers, including foreign ones, and there are sybaritic touches, like the large selection of cigars for sale. Live piano music from Thursday to Sunday evenings.
G6 Kärntner Ring 17 512 8998 Mon–Fri 7.30am–midnight, Sat–Sun 8.30am–midnight Trams 2, D to Schwarzenbergplatz

NEUE WIENER KÜCHE

Nouvelle cuisine arrived late in the city. The man chiefly responsible for its introduction was Werner Matt, a Tyrolean chef who came to the Hilton in the 1970s. As a result, *Selbstmord mit Gabel und Messer* (suicide by knife and fork; ▷ 5) subsided. Menus grew shorter, and the city's kitchens began to use more fresh produce to reduce flour, fat and deep-frozen ingredients.

CAFÉ SPERL (€€)

www.cafesperl.at
Established in 1880, this is one of the city's oldest and most authentic cafés.
E6 Gumpendorferstrasse 11 586 41 58 Mon–Sat 7am–11pm, Sun 11–8. Closed Sun Jul and Aug U1 to Karlsplatz, U2 to MuseumsQuartier, U4 to Kettenbrückengasse

GREEN COTTAGE (€€)

www.green-cottage.at
Close to Naschmarkt, this Chinese restaurant is remarkably successful at mingling European and Asiatic styles of cooking in an extremely creative menu. The ingredients (such as fillet of lamb or beef) may seem very Viennese, but the spicy gastronomic experience is from Sichuan.
E7 Kettenbrückengasse 3 586 6581 Mon–Sat 11.30–3, 6–11 U4 to Kettenbrückengasse

PIARISTENKELLER (€€€)

www.piaristenkeller.com
Crammed into the brick vaults of the Piarist

monastery, this restaurant is one of the most convivial in Vienna. It is decorated with flags, pictures and historic items. Don't miss the mildly Pythonesque hat parade, in which you may be invited to participate.
C4 Piaristengasse 45 406 01 93 Daily 6pm–midnight U2 to Rathaus Tram 2 to Lederergasse/Strozzigasse

RATHAUSKELLER (€€)

www.wiener-rathauskeller.at
In the huge neo-Gothic Rathaus (City Hall, ▷ 55), the restaurant's various rooms are decorated in Historicist style. It's big enough to escape the bus parties and the food is good.
D4 New City Hall, Rathausplatz 1/Felderstrasse 405 12 10 Mon–Sat 11.30–3, 6–11.30 U2 to Rathaus Trams 1, D to Burgtheater

RESTAURANT WIENER (€€)

www.restaurant-wiener.at
Friendly neighborhood *Beisl* (tavern), serving classic Austrian dishes like fried bread dumplings with egg, *Tafelspitz*, Wiener schnitzel and fried cheese. Good local wines.
C5 Hermanngasse 27A 524 52 52 Mon–Sat 5pm–2am, Sun 5pm–midnight U3 to Neubaugasse Bus 13A to Siebensterngasse; tram 49 to Neubaugasse

DAS SCHICK (€€€)

www.das-schick.at
This restaurant, located on the top floor of the Hotel Am Parkring, enjoys panoramic views over the rooftops of the city. It is a popular choice for special occasions and intimate dinner rendezvous.
G5 Hotel Am Parkring, Parkring 12 514 80 417 Mon–Fri 12–3, 6–10.30, Sat–Sun 6pm–10.30pm U3 to Stubentor Tram 2 to Weihburggasse

SCHNATTL (€€€)

www.schnattl.com
Enjoy modern and intensely inventive Viennese cuisine from the highly regarded chef Wilhelm Schnattl. Choose the degustation menu if you want to get a taste of several of his creations. There is a lovely courtyard dining area.
C4 Lange Gasse 40 405 3400 Mon–Fri 6pm–midnight U2 to Rathaus Trams 2, 46 to Lederergasse/Strozzigasse

THE *BEISL*

Most restaurants offering genuine Viennese cooking are carrying on the *Beisl* tradition: honest food, cooked and served in unpretentious surroundings. The word is of Yiddish origin (in the past, tavern keepers were often Jewish). Some *Beisls* have transformed into expensive restaurants, but many hold to tradition and keep their prices fair. Typical dishes include *Tafelspitz* (boiled beef), *Zwiebelrostbraten* (beefsteak with crispy onions) and *Beuschel* (chopped lung in sauce). Liver is also popular.

SLUKA (€€)

www.sluka.at
Another candidate for the title of Vienna's best patisserie, Sluka serves mouthwatering pastries and a tempting range of light lunches. Try some of the delicious petit fours or a slice of the melt-in-the-mouth Sachertorte.
D4 Rathausplatz 8 405 7172 Mon–Fri 8–7, Sat 8–5.30 Trams 1, D to Rathaus

ZU EBENER ERDE UND ERSTER STOCK (€€)

www.zu-ebener-erde-und-erster-stock.at
The Spittelberg area has many good eateries but this is the best, serving Viennese cooking with a light touch and much attention to seasonal specialties like asparagus. There's a very good wine list. The smarter restaurant part is upstairs, while the lower part is less pretentious; there is a good atmosphere in both areas.
D5 Burggasse 13 523 62 54 Mon–Fri 12–10 U2, U3 to Volkstheater

Apfelschnitte

Around Alsergrund

Alsergrund is a residential area dotted with palaces, churches and other places of interest, notably Sigmund Freud's home, where he lived for 47 years.

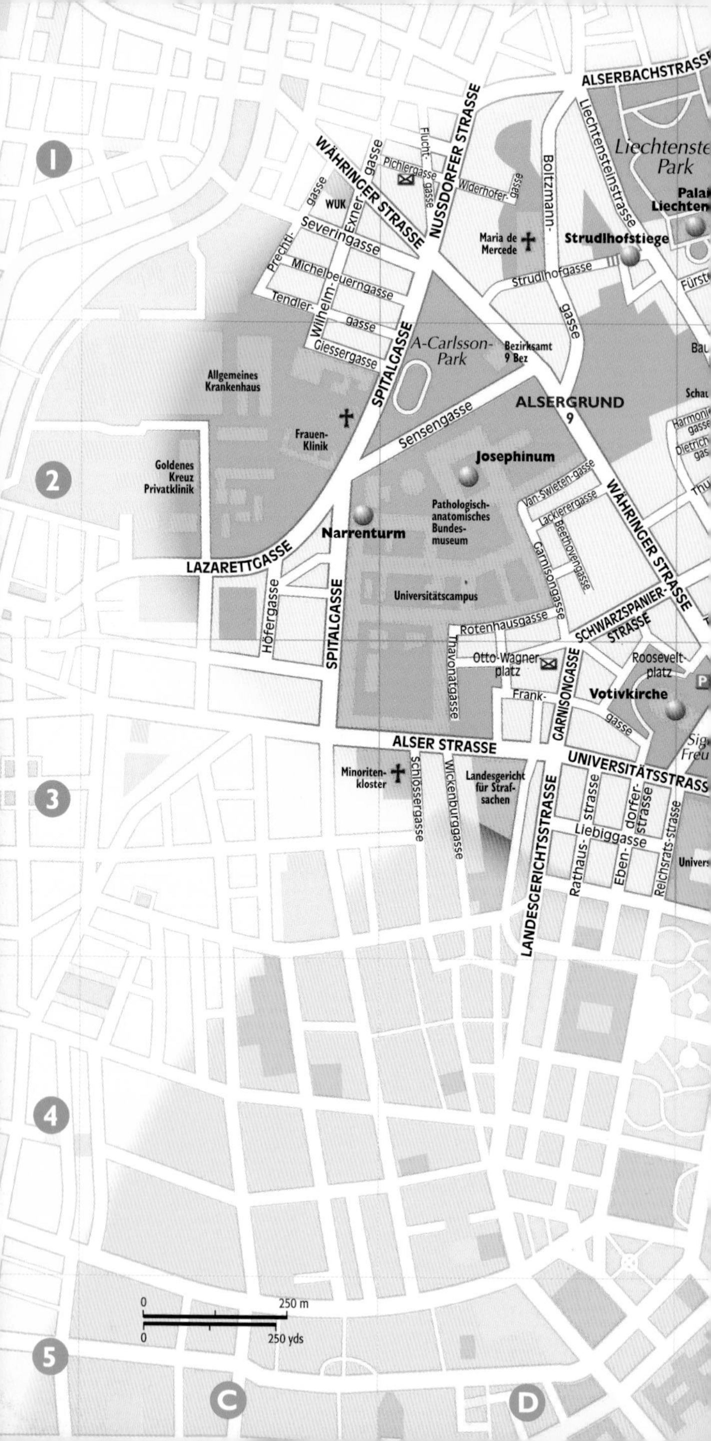

ALSERBACHSTRASSE
Liechtenstein Park
Liechtensteinstrasse
NUSSDORFER STRASSE
WÄHRINGER STRASSE
Flucht-gasse
Exner-gasse
Pichlergasse
Widerhofer-gasse
Boltzmann-gasse
WUK
Prechtl-gasse
Severingasse
Michelbeuerngasse
Tendler-gasse
Wilhelm-
Giessergasse
Maria de Mercede
Strudlhofstiege
Strudlhofgasse
A-Carlsson-Park
Bezirksamt 9 Bez
SPITALGASSE
Allgemeines Krankenhaus
Frauen-Klinik
Sensengasse
ALSERGRUND 9
Josephinum
Van-Swieten-gasse
Lackierergasse
Beethovengasse
Goldenes Kreuz Privatklinik
Narrenturm
Pathologisch-anatomisches Bundes-museum
Garnisongasse
LAZARETTGASSE
Höfergasse
Universitätscampus
Rotenhausgasse
SCHWARZSPANIER-STRASSE
Thavonatgasse
Otto-Wagner-platz
GARNISONGASSE
Roosevelt-platz
Votivkirche
Frank-gasse
ALSER STRASSE
Minoriten-kloster
Schlössergasse
Wickenburggasse
Landesgericht für Straf-sachen
LANDESGERICHTSSTRASSE
UNIVERSITÄTSSTRASSE
Rathaus-strasse
Liebiggasse
Eben-dorfer-strasse
Reichsrats-strasse
0
250 m
0
250 yds
1
2
3
4
5
C
D

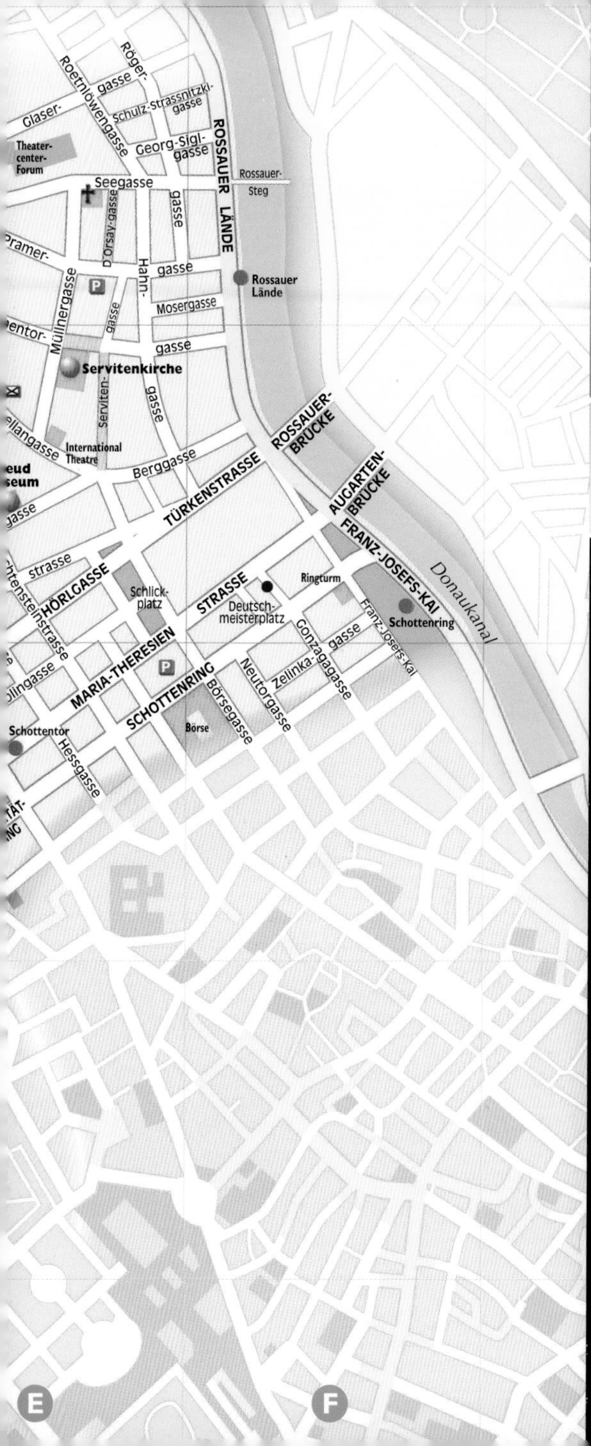

Around Alsergrund

Röger-gasse
Roetzlöwengasse
Glaser-
Schulz-Strassnitzki-gasse
Theater-center-Forum
Georg-Sigl-gasse
ROSSAUER LÄNDE
Rossauer-Steg
Seegasse
D'Orsay-gasse
gasse
Pramer-
Hahn-gasse
gasse
Rossauer Lände
Müllnergasse
gasse
Mosergasse
-entor-
gasse
Servitenkirche
Serviten-gasse
gasse
-liangasse
International Theatre
Berggasse
ROSSAUER-BRÜCKE
-eud -seum
TÜRKENSTRASSE
AUGARTEN-BRÜCKE
-gasse
FRANZ-JOSEFS-KAI
Donaukanal
strasse
-chtensteinstrasse
HÖRLGASSE
Schlick-platz
STRASSE
Ringturm
Deutsch-meisterplatz
Schottenring
Franz-Josefs-Kai
Gonzagagasse
Zelinka-gasse
MARIA-THERESIEN
-lingasse
SCHOTTENRING
Neutorgasse
Börsegasse
Börse
Schottentor
Hessgasse
-TÄT-
-ING
E
F

Freud Museum

TOP 25

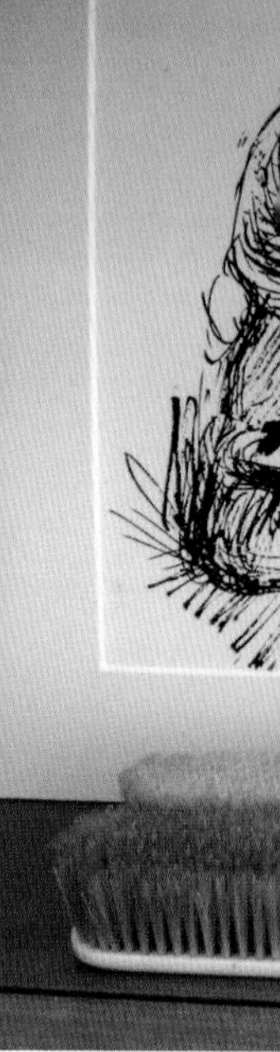

HIGHLIGHTS

- Freud's hat and cane hanging in the entrance hall
- Library
- Research Center
- Freud's antiques—he owned over 3,000

Some of the 20th century's most influential ideas stemmed from the tenant of No. 5, Berggasse 19, and it is interesting to see the place where his work began.

Sigmund Freud Recognized as the founder of modern psychoanalysis, Freud (1856–1939) was nonetheless typically Viennese, playing *tarock* (a card game still popular with the older generation), visiting Café Landtmann (▷ 62) and taking a daily constitutional along the entire length of the Ringstrasse. Most of his possessions are held in London, where he fled to escape Nazi persecution in 1938 (a year before his death). However, his youngest daughter, Anna, donated some items for display here, and his waiting room and the entrance hall

Clockwise from left: Decorative window; some of Freud's personal effects; inside Freud's apartment; outside the Freud Museum

appear as they would have done while he lived and worked in the apartment for almost half a century.

Theories Freud's most controversial theory was that infantile sexual impulses were at the root of adult neuroses. Adler and Jung—the other famous early psychoanalysts—parted company with him over this. However, many now-mainstream concepts started with Freud—for example, division of the personality into id and ego, and the ideas of sublimation and the Oedipus complex. Although many academics still accept Freud's dogmas as axiomatic, his critics believe that he doctored his evidence. The Viennese writer Karl Kraus, a contemporary of Freud's, remarked: "Psychoanalysis is the disease of which it purports to be the cure."

THE BASICS

www.freud-museum.at
E2
Berggasse 19
319 15 96
Daily 9–6
U2 to Schottentor
Tram D to Schlickgasse
None
Moderate

Palais Liechtenstein

TOP 25

Archway (left) in front of the Palais Liechtenstein (right)

THE BASICS

www.palaisliechtenstein.com
E1
Fürstengasse 1
319 57 67-153
Admission by guided tour only: Fri 3pm–4pm
Special "Baroque Dinner" evenings at the Garden Palace restaurant
U4 to Rossauer Lände
Bus 40A; tram D to Bauernfeldplatz
Good
Expensive
Tours require prebooking, either by phone or online

HIGHLIGHTS

- Badminton Cabinet, bought at auction in 2004 for a record-breaking 227 million euros
- Large series of Rubens paintings
- Baroque garden, reconstructed from old prints

This superbly renovated palace displays a major part of the artistic patrimony of the celebrated Liechtenstein family, rulers of the principality of the same name.

The Liechtensteins One of the oldest noble families of Europe, the Liechtensteins were first mentioned in 1136. They derive their name from Liechtenstein Castle, a stone's throw from Vienna. Elevated to princes in 1608, in 1719 they acquired their own sovereign state.

Garden Palace When Hitler invaded Austria in 1938, the Prince of Liechtenstein retreated to his own pocket-handkerchief state, taking his famous art collection with him. In 2004, part of that collection was returned to the family's Garden Palace (summer palace) in Vienna. A state-of-the-art gallery was created to make viewing as pleasurable and informal as possible so you feel you are enjoying the pictures as the Liechtensteins would themselves have done.

The collection No attempt has been made to stuff the rooms with as much art as possible, and the clear aim is to maximize the viewer's pleasure; if you want to know more there is a helpful audio guide. Note that opening hours are limited and prebooking is required. As well as masterpieces, ranging from Gothic to fin de siècle, the museum contains the Badminton Cabinet, which was originally made for an ancestor of the Duke of Beaufort by Florentine craftsmen in 1732.

More to See

JOSEPHINUM

Aspiring military surgeons pored over lifelike anatomical wax models here, preparing for a career on the battlefields of the Empire. The building now houses the Museum of Medical History.

D2 Währinger Strasse 25 40160-26000 Museum of Medical History: Fri–Sat 10–6. Closed hols Trams 37, 38, 40, 41, 42 to Sensengasse Inexpensive Guided tour in English Fri at 11am

NARRENTURM

The Narrenturm was used as an asylum until 1866; subsequently it housed a store and provided living quarters for medical staff. It is now the Museum for Pathology and Anatomy, and contains a large collection of medical curiosities.

C2 Corner of Sensengasse and Spitalgasse (up a zigzagging path) 406 86 72-2 Sep–Jul Wed 3–6pm, Thu 8am–11am, Sat 10–1. Closed hols U2 to Schottentor Tram 5 to Lazarettgasse; 43, 44 to Lange Gasse Inexpensive None Tours by arrangement

Josephinum

SERVITENKIRCHE

The fine cupola of the 17th-century Servite Church served as a prototype for other baroque churches in the city. A chapel inside is dedicated to the Servite St. Peregrine, who is invoked for healing lameness. The saint was a great benefactor of the poor, and special bread rolls are still distributed in the Servitengassse during the two-day St. Peregrine's fair in May.

E2 Servitengasse 9 317 61 95-0 Daily 8–7 U4 to Rossauer Lände Tram D to Schlickgasse Two steps Free

STRUDLHOFSTIEGE

This graceful art nouveau stairway with lanterns and wells was designed in 1910 by Theodor Jäger. The steps are especially attractive at night when lit by the stairway lanterns.

D1 Strudlhofgasse U4 to Rossauer Lände Tram D to Bauernfeldplatz

VOTIVKIRCHE

This huge neo-Gothic church was built to commemorate Emperor Franz Josef's escape from an assassination attempt in 1853. Its chapels are dedicated to Austrian regiments. Note the Renaissance sarcophagus of Count Salm, defender of Vienna in the Turkish siege of 1529.

D3 Rooseveltplatz 8 406 11 92-0 Thu–Sat 9–1, 4–6, Sun 9–1. Museum: Tue–Fri 4–6, Sat 10–1 U2 to Schottentor Trams 1, 2 to Schottentor Several steps Church free; museum inexpensive Holy Mass in English Sun at 11

Alsergrund Stroll

This is an attractive residential area of Vienna, dotted with a variety of churches, palaces and museums.

DISTANCE: 4km (2.5 miles) **ALLOW:** 2 hours without visits

START

SCHOTTENTOR

E3 U2 to Schottentor

Trams 1, 2

❶ Approach the overblown neo-Gothic Votivkirche (▷ 71) by walking through the Sigmund Freud Park opposite the Schottentor tram junction.

❷ On leaving the church, turn northeast onto Währinger Strasse. Continue to the next traffic lights, then take a right down Berggasse to the Freud Museum (▷ 68).

❸ Continue along Berggasse until the crossroads, then follow the lively Servitengasse to the Servitenkirche (▷ 71). You can enjoy good local fare at the Servitenwirt (▷ 75).

❹ From the Servitenkirche turn left and follow Grünentorgasse to the end and turn right on Porzellangasse. A few steps from here turn left for the Palais Liechtenstein (▷ 70).

❺ On leaving the palace courtyard, take two right turns.

❻ Cross Liechtensteinstrasse and climb the art nouveau steps of Strudlhofstiege (▷ 71). Take Boltzmanngasse to the left and cross Währinger Strasse for the Josephinum (Museum of Medical History, ▷ 71).

❼ From the Josephinum, take two right turns for Van-Swieten-Gasse. Once inside the university campus, follow the Leopold-Bauer-Weg to the Narrenturm (▷ 71), screened by trees to your right. Retrace Leopold-Bauer-Weg and continue through Courtyard 7 to Courtyard 1.

❽ Refreshment is available at several cheaper restaurants here. After leaving the campus by the exit to your left, return to Schottentor on foot or one stop on the tram.

SCHOTTENTOR

END

Shopping

DEMMERS TEEHAUS

www.tee.at

The genuine Chinese or Indian teas available here will please those who are dispirited by the tea bag and hot water that is sold as "tea" in cafés and restaurants of the notoriously coffee-bound Vienna. Not surprisingly, the founder and owner Andrew Demmer was born in London and returned with his parents from exile after World War II. There is a tea salon upstairs; choose from 250 types of tea.

E3 Mölkerbastei 5 533 59 95 Mon–Fri 9–6, Sat 9.30–1.30. Closed Jul–Aug. Tearoom Mon–Fri 10–6 U2 to Schottentor Buses 1A, 3A to Schottentor; trams 1, 2, D to Schottentor

FÜRNIS MÄDCHEN UND BUBEN

www.handpuppen.at

This shop began by importing and selling wooden toys from other countries and factories, but the owners felt that something was missing and decided to design toys themselves. Their soft, friendly dolls and animals are now exported to many countries. Other items for sale include sleeping bags, bookmarks—and much more.

E2 Servitengasse 4a 968 62 33 Mon–Fri 9.30–6.30, Sat 9.30–2 U4 to Rossauer Lände Tram D to Schlickgasse

TOSTMANN TRACHTEN

www.tostmann.at

This is the place to go for clothing with a *Tracht* (vernacular) look, for men, women and children. Choose between unobtrusive fashion or the full Monty. Every federal province of Austria has its own version of *Tracht*.

E3 Schottengasse 3A (corner to Mölkerbastei stairs) 533 53 31 Mon–Fri 10–6, Sat 10–5 U2 to Schottentor Buses 1A, 3A to Schottentor; trams 1, 2, D to Schottentor

UNGER UND KLEIN

www.ungerundklein.at

The best selection of wines from Lower Austria, Styria and Burgenland. Worth the detour also because of the interior by Eichinger oder Knechtl. They also have a daily wine offer designed to match the weather and your (or their) mood.

F3 Gölsdorfgasse 2 532 13 23 Mon–Fri 3–midnight, Sat 5–midnight U1, U4 to Schwedenplatz

NOT A CITY FOR BARGAINS

When Austria entered the European Union in 1995, it was thought prices would fall as a result of more penetration into a previously cartel-ridden and monopolists' market. In some areas (chiefly to do with food) this has happened, but in luxury goods, prices are similar to Munich or London and there are no bargains. Try to buy non-exclusive goods outside the Innere Stadt, where prices are higher because rents are high and many customers are well-to-do.

WAGNER WERKHAUS

A jumble of tableware, tablecloths, glasses, frames, door bells, lampshades and more.

E2 Servitengasse 8 31 01 573 Mon 3–6pm, Tue–Fri 10–1, 3–6, Sat 10–1 U4 to Rossauer Lände Tram D to Schlickgasse

XOCOLAT MANUFAKTUR

www.xocolat.at

This fine chocolate shop was opened under the guidance of top chef Christian Petz (who also runs the popular Holy-Moly! restaurant, ▷ 45). Chocolate bars and truffles are made on the premises—you can watch the chocolatiers as they work. There's also another branch in the shopping arcade at Freyung 2, Palais Ferstel.

E2 Servitengasse 5 310 00 20 Mon–Fri 10–6, Sat 10–1 U4 to Rossauer Lände Tram D to Schlickgasse

Also at E4 Freyung 2 535 43 63 Mon–Fri 9.30–6.30, Sat 10–6 U3 to Herrengasse

Entertainment and Nightlife

OPEN HOUSE THEATRE COMPANY

www.openhousetheatre.at

This is the successor to the now-defunct Vienna International Theatre. The Open House Theatre Company aims to bring high-level English-language theater to both the English-language community and locals who like to practice their English. Check online for performances during your visit. Note that while the company's offices are near Alsergrund, performances take place in theaters all over the city. Buy tickets over the phone or online.

Off map at D1 Döblinger Hauptstrasse 33A/20 680 225 12 90 Hours vary according to performance

PFARRKIRCHE LICHTENTAL

www.schubertkirche.at

Composer Franz Schubert was the greatest son of the Lichtental parish. The church where he was baptized, received his first exposure to music and where some of his great masses were first performed has hardly changed from his time. There are Schubert Days in late November and regular organ recitals at other times of the year.

Off map at D1 Marktgasse 40/Lichtentalergasse 315 26 46 U4 to Friedensbrücke Tram D to Althanstrasse

SUMMER STAGE

www.summerstage.at

From May to September Vienna's trendy Summer Stage along the Alsergrund Danube Canal is a magnet for young people. Viennese food and international fare is on offer, together with concerts and lectures, exhibitions, sporting facilities—and even a doggy watering hole with all canine comforts.

F1/2 Rossauer Lände south of Mosergasse 315 52 02 Daily 5pm–1am, Sun from 3pm U4 to Rossauer Lände

VOLKSOPER

www.volksoper.at

Even though it's in the uncongenial area of the *Gürtel* (Ring Road), the Volksoper is no poor relation of the Staatsoper. For visitors this is the best place to enjoy the operettas and some German operas hardly performed in the English-speaking world. For the locals it's a good place to see imported musicals and foreign-language operas in German. There are also ballet and solo performances, sometimes staged by the director himself. The Volksoper may not have the budget to engage internationally acclaimed opera stars, but like the English National Opera or the New York City Opera, it contributes something uniquely democratic to the city's musical scene. Needless to say the tickets also cost less.

C1 Währinger Strasse 78 51 444 36 70 U6 to Währinger Strasse-Volksoper Bus 40A; trams 40, 41, 42 to Währinger Strasse-Volksoper

WELL-KEPT SECRETS

Geheimtips—things that the initiates prefer to keep to themselves—are by definition inclined to be ephemeral. This page describes what might be called perennial *Geheimtips*—places that have established themselves as having something special to offer. They give a taste of Vienna beyond the superficial glitter it so willingly displays for tourists.

WUK

www.wuk.at

An arts area with a café and restaurant, also performance art, dance and DJ nights. Situated in a rundown former locomotive factory, the WUK has developed into one of Europe's largest and hottest art scenes, hosting 130 groups. The heart of Vienna's alternative culture, it focuses both on international trends and local innovations.

C1 Währinger Strasse 59 401 210 Mon–Fri 9–8, Sat–Sun 3–8pm. Hours vary according to events U6 to Währinger Strasse-Volksoper Trams 40, 41, 42 to Währinger Strasse-Volksoper

Restaurants

PRICES

Prices are approximate, based on a 3-course meal for one person.

€€€ over €40

€€ €20–€40

€ under €20

BERG (€€)

www.cafe-berg.at

A long-established café and restaurant for the gay community. Adjacent is the Löwenherz (Lionheart) bookshop with gay and feminist literature. Cool vibe in a modern setting; well known for its brunch (daily 10–3) and constantly changing menu.

E2 Berggasse 8/Wasagasse 319 57 20 Tue–Sat 10am–11pm, Sun 10–3 U2 to Schottentor Trams 37, 38, 40, 41 to Schwarzspanierstrasse

ETHIOPIAN RESTAURANT (€€)

www.members.aon.at/ethiopianrestaurant

Main dishes are served in a traditional style, with meats, spicy vegetables and condiments all piled atop a giant flattened piece of Ethiopian bread called *injera*. On Fridays and Saturdays they hold an Ethiopian coffee ceremony at 8.30pm.

D2 Währinger Strasse 15 40 20 726 Tue–Sat 11–11, Sun 3–11pm U2 to Schottentor Trams 37, 38, 40, 41 to Schwarzspanierstrasse

LA PASTERIA (€€)

www.lapasteria.at

Excellent Italian restaurant serving over 200 varieties of homemade pasta.

E2 Servitengasse 10 310 27 36 Mon–Fri 11–11 U4 to Rossauer Lände Tram D to Bauernfeldplatz

PORZELLAN (€€)

www.porzellan-lounge.at

Contemporary restaurant and bar serving Austrian and international cuisine. Try the *Grosses Erwachen* (Viennese breakfast)—bread rolls, ham, cheese and a poached egg.

E2 Servitengasse 2 315 63 63 Mon–Fri 8am–midnight, Sat–Sun 10am–midnight U2 to Schottentor Tram D to Schlickgasse

NO-FRILLS FOOD

Cynics say that the preferred dish of the Viennese is a big one. The new self-service restaurants, however, offer much more flexibility in terms of the size of portions and in the range of food (although the cuisine remains Austrian). Vienna's many historic wine vaults also offer local wines and modestly priced food in a convivial and romantic setting. Sandwich bars offer open-sandwiches, a specialty here, and markets always have stands selling snacks and delicacies.

RAGUSA (€€€)

www.ragusa.at

A seafood restaurant with fresh fish flown in daily from the Dalmatian coast of the Adriatic Sea. Full range of wines from Croatia. Italian cuisine also on offer.

E2 Berggasse 15 317 15 77 Mon–Fri 11.30–2.30, 6–11, Sat 6pm–11pm U2 to Schottentor Trams 37, 38, 40, 41 to Schwarzspanierstrasse

ROTH (€€)

www.kremslehnerhotels.at

A stylish restaurant offering Viennese classics such as *Tafelspitz* (boiled beef) and *Zwiebelrostbraten* (beef steak with crispy onions). Under the same management as the Hotel Regina—you can peek from the arcade into the latter's majestic former dining room.

E3 Währinger Strasse 1/Rooseveltplatz 402 79 95 Daily 12–12 U2 to Schottentor Trams 37, 38, 40, 41, 42, 43, 44 to Schottentor

SERVITENWIRT (€€)

www.servitenwirt.at

The full range of classic Viennese dishes, served in an unpretentious, traditional setting. They sell their own wine from Lower Austria.

E2 Servitengasse 7, beside Servite Church 315 23 87 Daily 11–11 U4 to Rossauer Lände Tram D to Schlickgasse Summer garden

Around Landstrasse, Wieden

This area features two of Europe's greatest baroque buildings: the Belvedere Palace and Karlskirche. Both palace and church, with their monumental architecture, have justly made the city renowned for its splendid late-flowering of the style.

5
6
7
8
9
E
F
G
Resselpark
Karlsplatz
Wien Museum
Karls-kirche
Hochstrahl-brunnen
Russian Liberation Monument
Palais-Schwarzenberg
Schwarzenberg-platz
Konzert-haus
Akademie-theater
LOTHRINGERSTRASSE
Lisztstrasse
Zaunergasse
Gardekirche
Museum für österreichische Kunst
Brucknerstrasse
Mattiellistrasse
Landesgericht f Zivilrecht
Paniglgasse
Karlsgasse
Frankenberg-gasse
Generali Found
GUSSHAUSSTRASSE
Schwindgasse
Wohllebengasse
Haus des Sports
PRINZ-EUGEN-STRASSE
Schwartzenberg-garten
Paulanergasse
FAVORITEN-STRASSE
Mozart-platz
Floragasse
Taubstummengasse
Argentinier-strasse
ORF Funkhaus
Plösslgasse
Schmöllerlgasse
Brahms-platz
MAYERHOFGASSE
Möllwald-platz
Danhauser-gasse
Diplomatische Akademie Theresianum
Akzent
Theresianumgasse
Waltergasse
BELVEDEREGASSE
St Elisabethplatz
St Elisabeth
Karolinengasse
Starhemberg-gasse
RAINERGASSE
FAVORITENSTRASSE
Viktorgasse
Goldeggasse
Mommsengasse
Argentinierstrasse
Weyringer-gasse
WIEDNER GÜRTEL
Andreas-Hofer-Denkmal
0
250 m
250 yds
HAUPTBAHN
FAVORIT
10

Sallinger-platz
Bayerngasse
Grimmelshausen-gasse
Gottfried-Keller-Gasse
Salesianer-gasse
Neuling-gasse
gasse
Strasse
gasse
Russische Kirche
Metternichgasse
Jaurès-gasse
Reisner
Linke Bahngasse
Rechte Bahngasse
Ungargasse
Unteres Belvedere
RENNWEG
Salesianerinnen-kloster
Rennweg
Stanislausgasse
Schützen-gasse
Belvederegarten
Praetorius-gasse
Magazin-gasse
Mechelgasse
Fasanplatz
RENNWEG
Aspangstrasse
Obere Bahngasse
Gerlgasse
Keilgasse
Göschlgasse
Joseph-Schmidt-platz
Schloss Belvedere
Botanischer Garten der Universität
Jacquingasse
Fasangasse
Hegergasse
Platz der Opfer der Deportation
Kölblgasse
Hohlweggasse
gasse
Khunngasse
Mohs-gasse
Kleist-gasse
Kärchergasse
Adolf-Blamauer-Gasse
Trubelgasse
Alpengarten
LANDSTRASSER GÜRTEL
Heinrich-Drimmel-platz
Schweizer Gartenstrasse
Heeresmuseumstrasse
Schweizergarten
Kelsenstrasse
ARSENALSTRASSE
Ghegastrasse
Museum des 20 Jahrhunderts
Heeresgeschichtliches Museum
H
J

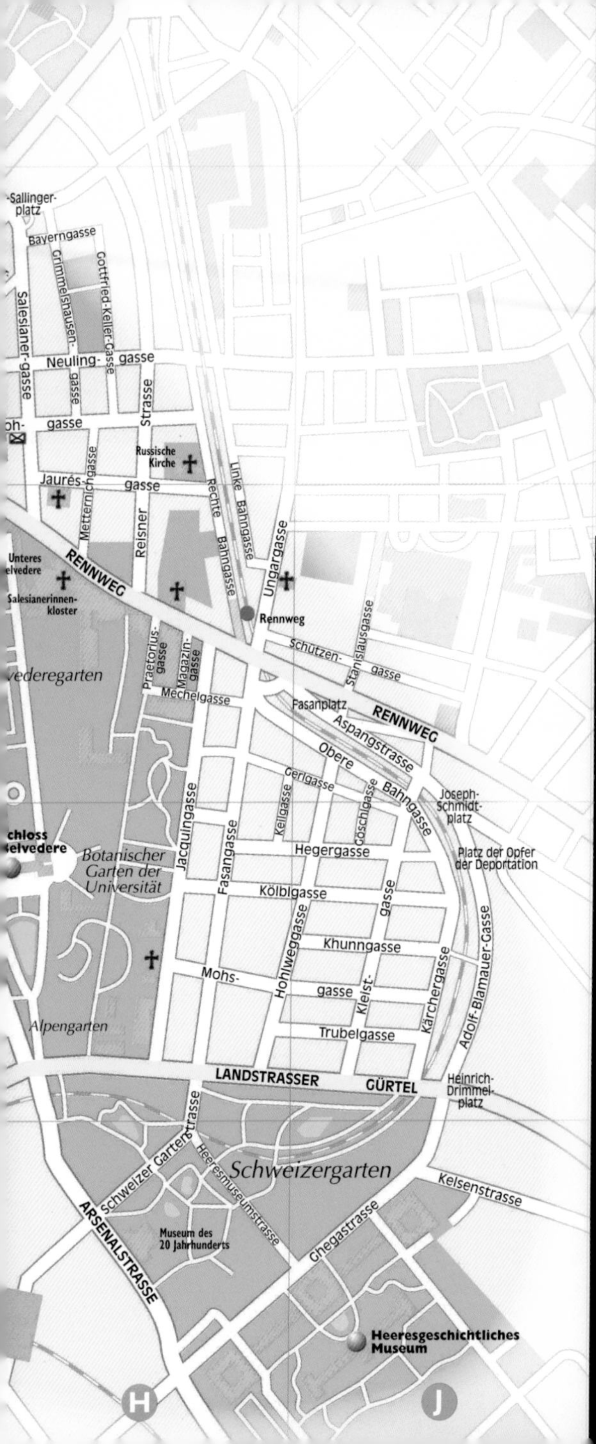

Heeresgeschichtliches Museum

The beautiful setting of the Museum of Military History (left); the car in which the Archduke was killed (right)

THE BASICS

www.hgm.at

J9

Arsenal Objekt 1

795 61-0

Daily 9–5. Closed 1 Jan, Easter Sun, 1 May, 1 Nov, 25, 31 Dec

Café

Bus 13A to Quartier Belvedere; trams O, D, 18 to Quartier Belvedere

Schnellbahn to Quartier Belvedere; U1 to Südtirolerplatz/ Hauptbahnhof

Good

Moderate; free first Sun of month

Audio guide

HIGHLIGHTS

- Ornate Byzantine facade

Ground floor

- *To the Unknown Soldier* (1916), Albin Egger Lienz
- Car in which Archduke Franz Ferdinand was assassinated
- Bloodstained uniform of Archduke Franz Ferdinand
- Tank park

The huge military complex known as the Arsenal and Museum of Military History is notable for its exotic pseudo-Byzantine architecture and for the collection inside, which provides visitors with a fascinating insight into Vienna's imperial history.

Riot-proof After the revolution of 1848, during which Am Hof, the old town armory, was plundered, leading Ringstrassen architects were commissioned to design a riot-proof arms factory and depot. This state-of-the-art complex was built with eight fortress-like barracks along its perimeter; by 1854 the facilities it enclosed were like those of an entire city within a city. The task of constructing it created jobs at a time of social unrest and unemployment. After World War II, part of the complex was rebuilt, and part is now occupied by state-owned drama workshops and the central telephone exchange, as well as the Museum of Military History.

Collection Themed sections include the Thirty Years War (1618–48), the Napoleonic Wars and the Austrian Navy (in existence until 1918). Particularly gruesome is the bloodstained tunic Archduke Franz Ferdinand, heir to the Habsburg throne, was wearing when he was assassinated in June 1914—an event that triggered the start of World War I. The museum also includes a display on "Republic and Dictatorship," which covers the period from the fall of the Habsburg Empire up to 1945.

St. Charles's Church at night (left); column symbolizing the Pillars of Hercules (middle); an angel statue (right)

TOP 25

Karlskirche

St. Charles's Church is one of Europe's finest baroque buildings. The symbolism in the two exotic columns at the front, fashioned on Trajan's Column in Rome, illustrates Habsburg secular power and spiritual legitimacy.

Origins In 1713 Vienna was hit by the last of many plagues; Emperor Charles VI vowed to dedicate a church to St. Charles Borromeo, who succored the people during the 1576 Milan plague. Begun in 1716, it is the masterpiece of Johann Bernhard Fischer von Erlach, who died in 1723, leaving his son, Joseph Emanuel, to complete it in 1739.

Paean in stone The two columns at the front symbolize the Pillars of Hercules in the Mediterranean, a reference to the Spanish realm (by then lost) of the other Habsburg line. Their spiraling friezes show the life of Charles Borromeo. The columns are also emblems of the Emperor's motto, *"Constantia et fortitudine."* The russet, gold and white interior creates a harmonious tranquility.

Paintings Austrian and Central European baroque is characterized by bright frescoes with transcendental motifs and the Karlskirche houses one of the most splendid examples. Johann Michael Rottmayr's painting soaring into the cupola shows the *Apotheosis of Charles Borromeo*. Among the other works is *Assumption of the Virgin* by Sebastiano Ricci.

THE BASICS

www.karlskirche.at

F6

Karlsplatz

504 61 87

Mon–Sat 9–6, Sun 12–7

U1, U2, U4 to Karlsplatz

Bus 4A to Karlsplatz; trams 1, 62 to Karlsplatz

Good

Moderate (cupola and Museo Borromeo included)

Audio guide

HIGHLIGHTS

- *Apotheosis of Charles Borromeo*, J. M. Rottmayr
- *Christ and the Centurion*, Daniel Gran
- *The Healing of the Man with the Palsy*, Giovanni Pellegrini
- Carved pulpit with rocaille and floral decoration

TIP

- It is possible to access the cupola to view the ceiling fresco close up and get a panoramic view of the city.

Schloss Belvedere

TOP 25

HIGHLIGHTS

Lower Belvedere
- Balthasar Permoser's statue of Prince Eugene

Upper Belvedere
- Sala Terrena with Hercules figures
- *The Kiss*, Gustav Klimt
- *Death and the Maiden*, Egon Schiele

TIP

- Visit the Botanical Garden and fragrant Alpine Garden adjacent to the gardens south of the Upper Belvedere.

After St. Stephen's Cathedral (▷ 31), the restored Belvedere Palace is Vienna's most important landmark. It was built in the early 18th century for Prince Eugene of Savoy, the most successful general in Austria's history.

Origins Lukas von Hildebrandt constructed the Lower Belvedere (Unteres Belvedere) between 1714 and 1716. The magnificent Upper Belvedere (Oberes Belvedere), designed to house the prince's fabulous art collection, was built between 1721 and 1723.

Palace in history Emperor Josef II installed the Imperial Picture Gallery in the Upper Belvedere. Franz Ferdinand, the heir to the throne, lived here from 1899 until his assassination in 1914.

Clockwise from far left: Grand staircase in the palace of the Upper Belvedere; statue of Atlas by Lorenzo Mattielli; the Lower Belvedere; view of the Upper Belvedere over the lake; The Judgment of Paris *by Max Klinger*

In 1955 the Austrian State Treaty ending the Allied occupation was signed in the Marble Hall.

Museums The Belvedere galleries underwent complete restructuring in 2007. The main entrance is now at the Lower Belvedere, which contains Prince Eugene's rooms, including the Golden Salon. The adjacent Orangery has been adapted for special exhibitions and the former stables display minor works of medieval art. Major medieval works and baroque paintings are now concentrated in the Upper Belvedere. However the main attraction remains the collection of masterpieces by Klimt, Schiele and Kokoschka, together with international art from the 19th century and later. Post-1945 art and the Fritz Wotruba collection are exhibited at 21er Haus in nearby Schweizergarten.

THE BASICS

www.belvedere.at

H8

Lower Belvedere: Rennweg 6; Upper Belvedere: Prinz-Eugen-Strasse 27

79 557-134 (tour information and booking)

Collections: daily 10–6 (Wed until 9). Stables: 10–noon. Shorter hours on 1 Jan, 24, 31 Dec. Alpine Garden: Apr–Jul 10–6

Café in Upper Belvedere

Tram 71 (Lower Belvedere), 0, 18 (Upper Belvedere), D (Upper and Lower belvederes)

Expensive

Good

Audio guide. Online ticket service

Wien Museum

TOP 25

Entrance to the Wien Museum (left); Lady in a Yellow Dress *by Max Kurzweil (right)*

THE BASICS

www.wienmuseum.at

F6

Karlsplatz

505 87 47

Tue–Sun 10–6. Closed 1 Jan, 1 May, 25 Dec

Café

U1, U2, U4 to Karlsplatz

Good

Moderate. Permanent exhibition free on first Sun of month

HIGHLIGHTS

- Eduard Fischer's maquette of the old town, 1854
- Franz Xaver Messerschmidt's grotesque busts
- *Stephansplatz* (1834), Rudolf von Alt
- Reconstructed apartment of playwright Franz Grillparzer
- Reconstructed sitting room in architect Adolf Loos's house
- *Anna Moll, Writing,* Carl Moll

Although housed in a drab 1950s-style building, the Viennese History Museum is one of Europe's best city museums, and its well-displayed contents bring the Viennese past vividly to life.

Origins The characterless design of the structure—its banality made more striking by its juxtaposition with the baroque architecture of St. Charles's Church next door—aroused much anger among Viennese patriots, although it had its defenders.

Museum collection Vienna's history, topography, art and culture are explored in the many works of art and architectural relics, and in the early city plans, reconstructions of interiors like Adolf Loos's living room and Franz Grillparzer's Biedermeier apartment, and beautifully made period models of the city.

Sweeping view The ground floor spans prehistory (Hallstatt culture) up to and including medieval times. On the first floor are exhibits of the baroque period and Enlightenment. The material relating to the time of the Turkish siege of Vienna (weapons and a portrait of Turkish commander Kara Mustafa) is of particular interest.

Renovation There are plans to close the museum temporarily to allow for renovation. Check beforehand that it is open when you intend to visit.

More to See

HOCHSTRAHLBRUNNEN

In 1873, a huge fountain was built at the southern end of Schwarzenbergplatz in front of Schwarzenberg Palace to mark the opening of Vienna's first water supply from the Alpine peaks (*Hochquellenleitung*). It brought fresh water to the city from 90km (56 miles) away. The fountain is illuminated at night.

G6 Schwarzenbergplatz Trams D to Gusshausstrasse, 71 to Am Heumarkt

PALAIS-SCHWARZENBERG

In 1716, Prince Schwarzenberg bought an unfinished palace by Lukas von Hildebrandt and then commissioned Johann Bernhard Fischer von Erlach, and later his son Joseph Emanuel, to complete the structure, which is still owned by the family. The grand sweep up to the portico was conceived by the younger Fischer, who also installed Vienna's first steam-driven motor to pump water for the fountains. The Schwarzenbergs' neighbor and rival, Prince Eugene of Savoy, had to postpone his great Schloss Belvedere project (▷ 82–83) until he had persuaded the Schwarzenbergs to sell a vital piece of adjacent land.

G7 Schwarzenbergplatz 9 No access to palace and garden Tram D to Gusshausstrasse

RUSSIAN LIBERATION MONUMENT

Just behind the Hochstrahlbrunnen, this massive memorial to the Soviet Red Army recalls the period just after World War II when Vienna was divided into four occupation zones, each controlled by one of the Allied powers (Britain, France, the US and the Soviet Union). The monument, a white marble colonnade encircling a large statue of a Red Army soldier, dates from 1945 and recalls the 17,000 Red Army soldiers who fell in the battle for Vienna in April that year.

G6 Schwarzenbergplatz Trams D to Gusshausstrasse, 71 to Am Heumarkt

The Russian Liberation Monument

Baroque at its Best

Karlskirche and the Belvedere Palace, with its gardens and fine collection of Secessionist art, are the highlights of this walk.

DISTANCE: 4km (2.5 miles) **ALLOW:** 2 hours without visits

START

KARLSPLATZ

F6 U1, U2, U4 to Karlsplatz

❶ From the underground passage connecting the Opera and Karlsplatz, take the Resselpark exit to the south. On your left you will see the Karlsplatz pavilions designed by Otto Wagner, while ahead rises Karlskirche (▷ 81).

❷ On leaving the church, turn south into Argentinierstrasse. At the second crossroads turn left and approach Schwarzenbergplatz through Gusshausstrasse.

❸ Cross Prinz-Eugen-Strasse to the Hochstrahlbrunnen (▷ 85) and the Russian Liberation Monument (▷ 85). Bear right into Rennweg.

❹ Then continue up Rennweg to the entrance of the Belvedere Palace (▷ 82–83) and museums. Having viewed the Lower Belvedere, walk up the sloping gardens to the Upper Belvedere.

❺ Visit the Upper Belvedere, with its collections of art, and enjoy the view of Vienna from the upper windows.

❻ On leaving the Belvedere, bear right round the building and head for the Alpine Garden to your left. After visiting the garden, retrace your steps through the Belvedere's southern garden as far as the Gürtel (Ring Road), which you cross to reach the Schweizergarten.

❼ Take the path to the left of the ornamental pool and continue along the promenade. After refreshment in the Schweizergarten restaurant, head up Heeresmuseum Strasse to visit the Heeresgeschichtliches Museum (▷ 80).

❽ On leaving the museum through the main gate, turn left into Ghegastrasse and then right into Arsenalstrasse.

END

HAUPTBAHNHOF

H9 U1 to Südtirolerplatz/ Hauptbahnhof

Shopping

ALOIS FRIMMEL

www.knopfkoenig.at

This shop, founded in 1884, sells only buttons. Maybe the "old king of buttons" has precisely the one you have been trying to find for years.

F7 Zum alten Knopfkönig, Wiedner Hauptstrasse 34 587 92 68 Mon–Wed 10–4.45, 5.15–6, Fri 10–3.45, 4.15–6, Sat 10–1 Tram 62 to Paulanergasse

BADER & PARTNER

www.bader-partner.at

Balloons and all kinds of display and party products.

F7 Wiedner Hauptstrasse 36 202 6660-0 Mon–Fri 9–6.30 Tram 62 to Mayerhofgasse

BAHNHOFCITY

www.hauptbahnhofcity.wien

With the opening of the new Main Train Station at the end of 2014 came the addition of the city's newest and one of its largest shopping malls. The Bahnhofcity shopping center has some 90 stores spread out over 20,000sq m (215,300sq ft) of floor space. Stores include major clothing, design and electronics outlets. In addition, there is a branch of the city tourist office, as well as banks, restaurants and places to pick up food or drink for the train journey.

H9 Wien Hauptbahnhof, Am Hauptbahnhof 1 05 1717 Daily 9–9 U1 to Südtirolerplatz/Hauptbahnhof

EDI-BÄR

www.edibaer.at

Margit Edinger sells and restores teddy bears, as well as other soft toys. There are homemade glass bracelets and other jewelry, and typically Viennese petit-point bags.

J5 Landstrasser Hauptstrasse 28 710 25 84 Tue–Fri 10–1, 2–6, Sat 10–1 U3 Rochusgasse Tram O to Sechskrügelgasse

LUDWIG REITER

www.ludwigreiter.at

Founded in 1885, this shoemaker maintains a Viennese tradition of solid and comfortable shoes of the finest quality. Reiter has developed a wide range of casual shoes, fine leather goods and other accessories.

The shop's exclusivity is reflected both in the price and quality of the merchandise.

F7 Wiedner Hauptstrasse 41 505 82 58 Mon–Fri 9.30–6, Sat 9.30–5. Closed Sat in Jul, Aug Trams 1, 62 to Mayerhofgasse

TRACHTENMODE

The basis of traditional Austrian dress is peasant and hunting costume. Women wear *Dirndls*—dresses with full skirts and lace blouses with a tight, revealing bodice—perhaps topped by a velvet jacket. Men wear green cloth jackets with braided cuffs and lapels, sometimes with buttons made from antlers. The best *Trachtenmode* is normally reserved for special occasions such as festivals and dances.

MARIOL

www.mariol.info

In this shop women can measure up for "chic from size 42 upwards," which means appealing clothes for those whose figures won't make the catwalk. You are welcome to make appointments outside the ordinary opening times. It's a place that sells personal style as much as clothes.

J5 Landstrasser Hauptstrasse 28 Mon–Fri 10–6, Sat 10–3. Outlet: Tue 10–6 713 69 60 U3 to Rochusgasse Bus 4A to Rochusgasse; tram O to Sechskrügelgasse

PISCHINGER

www.pischinger.at

The eponymous chocolatier offers his own products, one of which is a Viennese classic, the Pischinger Eck—a dark chocolate triangle with the original Pischinger nut-croquant-filling. The business has been running since 1849.

H9 Wien Hauptbahnhof, Am Hauptbahnhof 1 Mon–Fri 9–9, Sat–Sun 10–6 U1 to Südtirolerplatz/Hauptbahnhof

Entertainment and Nightlife

ARNOLD SCHÖNBERG CENTER

www.schoenberg.at

Not only a concert hall, but also an archive library and exhibition hall dedicated to the founder of Viennese modernism.

G6 Schwarzenbergplatz 6 712 18 88 Trams D, 2, 71 to Schwarzenbergplatz

KONZERTHAUS

www.konzerthaus.at

Opened in 1913, the building contains three concert halls: the Grosser Saal, for orchestral performances; and the Mozartsaal and Schubertsaal for chamber music, modern music and *Lieder* evenings. In summer there are twice-weekly selections of Mozart's music, played by musicians dressed in period costume.

G6 Lothringerstrasse 20 242 002 U4 to Stadtpark

MUSIKVEREIN

www.musikverein.at

The Musikverein is famous for its superb acoustics and sumptuous gilded interior. The Wiener Philharmoniker's New Year's Day Concert is broadcast from here and the orchestra's Sunday concerts are a Viennese institution. During the week there are orchestral concerts in the Great Hall, and chamber music in the Brahmssaal.

F6 Bösendorferstrasse 12 505 81 90 for tickets U1, U2, U4 to Karlsplatz Trams 1, D to Kärntner Ring

PALACES

The city's summer music festival, Wiener Musik-Sommer, offers graceful chamber music in some lovely baroque palaces, among them Palffy and Auersperg.

RADIOKULTURHAUS

www.radiokulturhaus.orf.at

All kinds of music, often in virtuoso performances, may be heard in the Austrian Broadcasting Company's (ORF) Broadcasting Hall or in the adjacent Kulturcafé.

MUSICAL TASTE

The Musikverein—concert hall for the Society of the Friends of Music—was founded in the 19th century. Mainstream Viennese taste is conservative: "The popularity of Brahms," wrote one critic, "is due largely to his music being exactly suited to Viennese tastes, not too hot and not too cold; it eschews excitement and seldom commits the unforgivable sin of being boring." But there has always been a radical element. The greatest scandal in the Musikverein's history was in 1913 when pro- and antimodernists began fighting at a Schönberg concert.

F7 Argentinierstrasse 30a 501 70 377 U1 to Taubstummengasse Tram D to Plösslgasse

SCHWARZBERG

www.ostklub.at

An enormous venue devoted to a diverse program of music from around the world. Evenings could involve piano music, French chansons, folk or flamenco.

G6 Schwartzenbergplatz 10/1 505 62 28 Tue–Thu 8pm–2am, Fri–Sat 8pm–4am U1, U2, U4 to Karlsplatz Tram 1 to Karlsplatz

THERESIANUM

www.wieneroperettensommer.at

A tradition of Best-of-Operetta revues has been established at the historic open-air stage in the garden of another former Habsburg summer palace.

F7 Favoritenstrasse 15 505 35 26-0 U1 to Taubstummengasse

URANIA

www.planetarium-wien.at

Max Fabiani's interesting late Jugendstil building on the Danube Canal was restored a few years ago. A multicultural performance hall, it hosts cinema and puppet theater and has an observatory.

H4 Uraniastrasse 1 89 174 150-000 U1, U4 to Schwedenplatz Trams 1, 2 to Schwedenplatz

Restaurants

PRICES

Prices are approximate, based on a 3-course meal for one person.

€€€ over €40

€€ €20–€40

€ under €20

BODEGA ESPAÑOLA (€)

www.bodegaespaniola.at

A taste of Spain in the heart of Vienna's Fourth District. Wash down tapas like *pinchos de pollo con arroz* (skewers of grilled chicken on rice) with a good choice of Spanish wines. There's an open fire in winter.

G8 Belvedergasse 10 504 55 00 Mon–Sat 6pm–1am Tram D to Schloss Belvedere

CASA ALBERTO (€)

www.casa-alberto.at

An Italian restaurant popular with journalists from the nearby ORF (Austrian Broadcasting Company).

F7 Argentinierstrasse 15 505 71 76 Daily 11am–midnight U1 to Taubstummengasse Tram D to Gusshausstrasse

KLEIN STEIERMARK (€)

A relaxing informal hostelry offering specialties from the province of Styria. Try the *Mistfuhre* (literally: "a load of rubbish"), which consists of grilled and fried meat with vegetables. In summer the garden with adjacent playground is ideal for a family outing.

H9 Heeresmuseumstrasse 1 (in the Schweizergarten) 799 58 83 Daily 11–11 (winter Sun 11–10); 25, 26 Dec 11–3. Closed 24 Dec and about 2 weeks after Christmas U1 to Südtirolerplatz/Hauptbahnhof Trams O, 18 to Fasangasse

SALM BRÄU (€)

www.salmbraeu.com

Bustling beer cellar in a former monastery. Good-value hot and cold food and great beer, some brewed on the premises.

H7 Rennweg 8 799 599 92 Daily 11am–midnight Tram 71 to Unteres Belvedere

SPERL (€€)

www.restaurant-sperl.at

A reliable restaurant offering a first-class selection of Viennese food. Specialties are the beef classics; try the roasted sirloin with onions (*Wiener Rostbraten*). The intimate garden is a romantic place to go in summer.

G8 Karolinengasse 13/Mommsengasse 504 73 34 Mon–Thu 10.30–10.30, Fri–Sun 11–11. Closed 2 weeks after Christmas Bus 13A; tram D to Schloss Belvedere

WAITERS

While the service in Vienna's top restaurants is assiduous and fast, in less expensive establishments that may not always be the case. The joke is that the commonest phrase to be heard in a Viennese coffeehouse is: "My colleague will be with you immediately." However even when their service is slow, Viennese waiters are quick-witted and full of repartee.

STADTPARK BRÄU (€€)

www.stadtparkbraeu.at

Popular, rustic beer joint that's beloved by locals for the Austrian version of comfort food: schnitzels, goulash and *tafelspitz* (boiled beef). There's a large nonsmoking section. It's best to reserve a table in advance as it gets pretty crowded.

H5 Am Heumarkt 5 713 71 02 Daily 11am–midnight U4 to Stadtpark

STEIRERECK (€€€)

www.steirereck.at

A distinguished restaurant in stunning premises in the Stadtpark, famous for the delicacy of its *Neue Wiener Küche* and its well-chosen wine list. Reserve in advance. The bar, Meierei, serves dairy-based snacks and light meals.

H5 Am Heumarkt 2 713 31 68 Restaurant: Mon–Fri 11.30–3, 6.30–11. Bar: Mon–Fri 8am–11pm, Sat–Sun 9–7. Closed hols U3 to Stubentor or Landstrasse, U4 to Stadtpark (park exit)

Vienna's suburbs were once home ground both for the nobility and for craftsmen, with residential areas, cemeteries and workshops. Just beyond them lies the varied landscape of the Wienerwald and the water meadows of the Danube's floodplain.

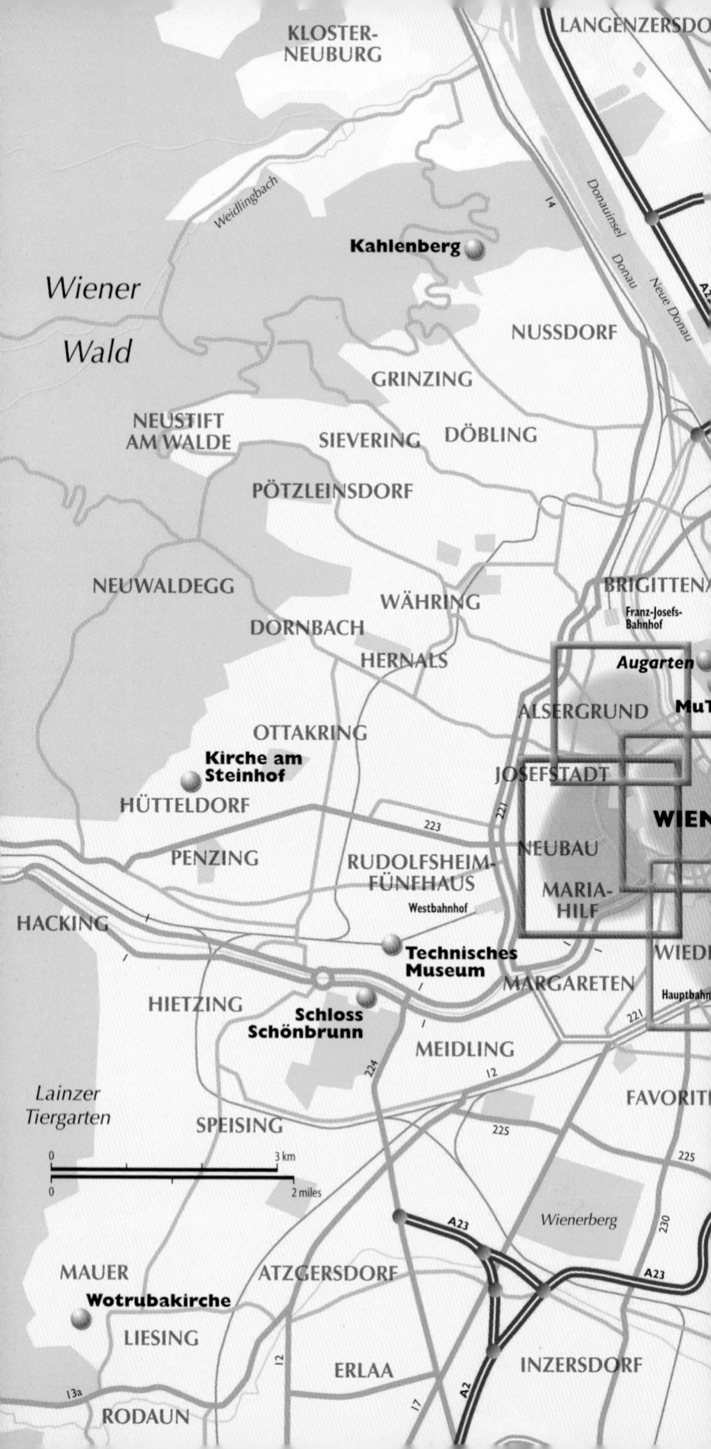
KLOSTER-
NEUBURG
LANGENZERSDO
Weidlingbach
Kahlenberg
14
Donauinsel
Donau
Neue Donau
Wiener
Wald
NUSSDORF
GRINZING
NEUSTIFT
AM WALDE
SIEVERING
DÖBLING
PÖTZLEINSDORF
NEUWALDEGG
BRIGITTENA
Franz-Josefs-
Bahnhof
WÄHRING
DORNBACH
HERNALS
Augarten
ALSERGRUND
MuT
OTTAKRING
Kirche am
Steinhof
JOSEFSTADT
HÜTTELDORF
221
223
WIEN
NEUBAU
PENZING
RUDOLFSHEIM-
FÜNFHAUS
MARIA-
HILF
Westbahnhof
HACKING
Technisches
Museum
WIED
MARGARETEN
Hauptbahn
HIETZING
Schloss
Schönbrunn
221
MEIDLING
224
12
Lainzer
Tiergarten
FAVORIT
SPEISING
225
0
3 km
225
0
2 miles
Wienerberg
A23
230
MAUER
ATZGERSDORF
A23
Wotrubakirche
LIESING
12
ERLAA
INZERSDORF
13a
A2
17
RODAUN

GERASDORF BEI WIEN
REBERSDORF
GROSS-JEDLERSDORF
NEUSÜSSENBRUNN
FLORIDSDORF
LEOPOLDAU
BREITENLEE
KAGRAN
DONAUSTADT
Alte Donau
HIRSCH-STETTEN
Gänsehäufel
KAISER-MÜHLEN
Donau
STADLAU
Prater &
Riesenrad
LEOPOLDSTADT
ASPERN
KunstHausWien
Hundertwasser-Haus
Wittgenstein Haus
LANDSTRASSE
Wiener
Strassenbahnmuseum
Donauinsel
Neue Donau
Lobau
Donau
ALBERN
SIMMERING
Bestattungsmuseum
ROTH-
EUSIEDL
OBERLAA
A22
A23
A4
S2
302
225
10
3
3b
7
8
11

Danube Cruise

TOP 25

Cruising the Danube near Reichsbrücke (left); tour boat on the Donaukanal (right)

THE BASICS

M1

Vienna Cruises

www.ddsg-blue-danube.at

58 880

Departures daily from Schwedenbrücke. Winter break (Nov–Mar)

Expensive

Twin City Liner

www.twincityliner.com

58 880

Several departures daily from Schwedenbrücke. Weekends only mid-Oct to Dec; winter break Jan to mid-Mar

Good; advance reservation essential

Expensive

Advance reservations recommended. See website for departures and border formalities for Slovakia

NationalparkBoot

4000-49495 (booking required)

2 May–26 Oct daily at 9 near Salztorbrücke. Cruise is 4 hours with 1 hour walk

Moderate

HIGHLIGHTS

- UNO-City (the towering UN headquarters building)
- Kahlenberg and other hills
- The Secessionist Nussdorf Lock and Lock House

Traditional Danube cruises start at Schwedenplatz, from a striking ferry station designed to look like a boat. The route begins in the Donaukanal, then turns up the main river with a stop at the Reichsbrücke. It continues to Nussdorf and returns down the Donaukanal.

River cruises There are also special cruises, mainly in the evenings, offering music and dancing. Also leaving from the northwestern end of Schwedenplatz (at Salztorbrücke) is the NationalparkBoot, which takes you to the Danube National Park and its water meadows. The park begins inside the city's boundaries and extends as far as the Slovak border.

Twin City Liner A cruise on the Twin City Liner is an experience worth having. In little more than an hour, this huge catamaran rushes you to Bratislava, capital of the Slovak Republic. It costs twice the price of the train journey but you start and arrive right in the heart of both cities.

Donauinsel The artificial island between the Old and the New Danube has become popular for biking, picnicking and (at its southern tip) for nudism. One weekend in June each year, the island hosts what is said to be Europe's biggest outdoor festival of pop music (free access). There are modestly priced restaurants with international cuisine around the "Copa Cagrana" between U1 stations Donauinsel and Kaisermühlen VIC.

Hundertwasser-Haus (left); KunstHausWien (right)

TOP 25

Hundertwasser-Haus and KunstHausWien

Hundertwasser's career as an amateur architect began with his now-famous Hundertwasser-Haus in Vienna's Third District. It was built with the help of a professional architect, Josef Krawina, and opened in 1985.

The artist Born Friedrich Stowasser in 1928, the partly Jewish artist survived Nazi persecution in his native city of Vienna. In 1949, he took the name "Friedensreich Hundertwasser" and in 1953 painted the first of his colorful spirals. Over the years he became more and more involved in ecological initiatives as part of his artistic credo. He died on board the *Queen Elizabeth II* following a trip to New Zealand in 2000 and was buried there in his Garden of the Happy Dead—without a coffin, but with a tulip tree planted above his remains.

Hundertwasser-Haus The building reflects his opposition to pure functionalism and his view that "the straight line is godless." The house is not accessible (it's a block of flats). Instead, "Hundertwasser Village" across the street offers visitors the full Hundertwasser experience in all its whimsicality. There are souvenir shops, a bar and a restaurant with a pleasant garden terrace.

KunstHausWien The KunstHaus is in a former furniture factory close to the Hundertwasser-Haus. It was refurbished by the artist and now offers a survey of his life and work. Exhibitions pay homage to his unconventionality.

THE BASICS

Hundertwasser-Haus

www.hundertwasserhaus.info

J4

Kegelgasse 34/Löwengasse 41

View from outside only

Tram 1 to Hetzgasse

Good

KunstHausWien

www.kunsthauswien.com

J4

Untere Weissgerberstrasse 13

712 04 91

Daily 10–7

Café-restaurant

Trams 1, O to Radetzkyplatz

Good; ask at ticket office

Moderate

TIP

- You can cruise the Danube from Schwedenplatz in MS *Vindobona*, renovated by Hundertwasser in 1995.

Kahlenberg

TOP 25

Karl-Marx-Hof (left); a Heuriger *or wine tavern (right)*

THE BASICS

See map ▷ 92
U4 to Heiligenstadt then bus 38A
Beethoven Houses
Testament Museum:
Probusgasse 6
Tue–Sun 10–1, 2–6
Restaurant Mayer:
Pfarrplatz 2
Sun–Fri from 4pm, Sat and hols from 11am
Tram 37 to Geweygasse
Secessionist Villa Colony
Steinfeldgasse 2, 4, 6, 7; Wollergasse 10
Tram 37 to Hohe Warte

HIGHLIGHTS

- View from Kahlenberg
- Karl-Marx-Hof tenement block

TIP

- The Heurigen Express (www.heurigenexpress.at) is an open-top hop-on/hop-off shuttle bus connecting Nussdorf (Tram D) and Kahlenberg (Apr–Oct daily 12–6 every hour, moderate). It also goes to Melk and the Wachau Valley (▷ 104).

If you've had enough of culture, head to the hills north of the city, drink some wine in one of the villages and still see some fine architecture along the way.

Kahlenberg Imperial troops and their allies gathered here before liberating Vienna from the Turkish siege in 1683. The hill has become the most popular place from which to view the panorama of Vienna. In the diminutive Sobieski Chapel a fresco recalls the Polish contribution to the liberation of Vienna.

Heiligenstadt Heiligenstadt is famous for the Heiligenstadt Testament, a letter written by an ailing Beethoven to his brothers. If this depresses you, restore your spirits with a glass of wine in the Beethoven House on Pfarrplatz.

Hohe Warte Secessionist Villa Colony Josef Hoffmann was a leading light of the Vienna Secession and cofounder of the Wiener Werkstätte. Four of his villas are located above Heiligenstadt's St. Michael's Church.

Karl-Marx-Hof Opposite the Heiligenstadt U-Bahn station is the most impressive dwelling-house of the 1920s "Red Vienna" period. Over 1km (0.6 miles) in length, it is the longest residential building in the world and once held 1,382 apartments. Many of these "workers' fortresses" played a significant role in the 1934 Civil War between authoritarian Conservative and Social Democratic forces.

The MuTh building is a combination of existing baroque structures and modern architecture

TOP 25

MuTh

The MuTh (Musik and Theater) opened at the end of 2012 as a concert hall for classical music and music theater. It's now also the permanent home of the Vienna Boys' Choir.

Vienna Boys' Choir Arguably the best-known choir of its kind in the world, the Wiener Sängerknaben was established more than 500 years ago as a church choir for Emperor Maximilian I. It has around 100 singers, from 10 to 14 years of age. Members come from Austria and around the world. The choir is divided into four touring groups, named after famous composers: Bruckner, Haydn, Mozart and Schubert.

Repertoire In the past, the choir performed mainly sacred and classical music, but in recent years the group has come under some pressure to diversify and modernize its repertoire. These days, expect anything from traditional Mozart and Haydn to pop and world music, such as a series of performances of Native American music. In addition to the MuTh, the choir regularly performs at the Vienna State Opera (▷ 35) and Burgkapelle (▷ 26). See the website www.wienersaengerknaben.at for an updated performance schedule.

MuTh As well as hosting the Vienna Boys' Choir, the MuTh offers a wide-ranging program of classical music, modern dance, ballet and much more. Many performances are aimed at younger audiences.

THE BASICS

www.muth.at;
www.wienersaengerknaben.at

G1

Am Augartenspitz 1 (corner of Castellezgasse)

347 80 80-1020

Box office: Mon–Fri 4pm–6pm

U2 to Taborstrasse

Tram 2 to Taborstrasse, tram 31 to Obere Augartenstrasse

Some wheelchair spaces

Moderate

TIP

- Try to book your tickets as far in advance as possible as Vienna Boys' Choir performances are very popular.

Prater and Riesenrad

TOP 25

Rides at the funfair on Prater (left and right)

THE BASICS

www.prater.at;
www.wienerriesenrad.com
K2
East of Praterstern
729 20 00
Funfair: 15 Mar–Oct daily. Ferris Wheel: May–Sep daily 9am–11.45pm; Mar–Apr, Oct 10–9.45; Nov–Feb 10–7.45 (book online). Closed 24, 31 Dec. *Liliputbahn*: daily 10–7
U1, U2 to Praterstern
Trams O, 5 to Praterstern
Good
Ferris Wheel: moderate; *Liliputbahn*: inexpensive. Combined tickets available

HIGHLIGHTS

- Ferris wheel
- *Liliputbahn*

TIP

- Take the *Liliputbahn* to Stadion, stroll down the Hauptallee and enjoy food at the Lusthaus (closed Wed).

The former imperial hunting grounds were opened to the public in 1766, and now include a chestnut avenue, a fairground and other leisure facilities. The world-famous amusement park has many diversions: the *Riesenrad* (Ferris wheel) is among the best known and most popular.

The big wheel The Giant Ferris Wheel on the Prater, built in 1896 by Englishman Walter Basset, was where Harry Lime, played by Orson Welles, met his old friend in the film *The Third Man*. The wheel rotates at 75cm (29in) per second and offers great views across the city. Compartments can be hired for private celebrations and you can even get married in one.

Amusement park There has been ongoing debate between the entrepreneurs of the different attractions and the City of Vienna regarding the future of the "Wurstelprater" funfair. Some wish to retain its traditional character, others want to modernize it. In fact traditional and new elements can be found here. Attractions include the *Geisterbahn* (ghost train), the old-fashioned *Ringelspiel* (merry-go-round) and the narrow-gauge *Liliputbahn* (381mm/15in), which starts from just behind the Giant Ferris Wheel. There are new dodgems and various "test your strength" booths. Adherents of old and new meet on the neutral ground of the *Schweizerhaus* (Swiss House) to sample its notoriously gigantic *Stelze* (knuckle of pork) served with Czech beer.

The imposing facade of Schloss Schönbrunn (left); view of the palace from the formal gardens (right)

TOP 25

Schloss Schönbrunn

Schönbrunn is an impressive, if slightly cold, palace, which was designed to show how many rooms a great monarch could afford. Yet Maria Theresa (1740–80) made it a cheerful home for her 12 surviving children. The palace and park are now a UNESCO World Heritage Site.

Pacassi's palace The original designs for an imperial residence in the hunting park with the beautiful spring (the *schöner Brunn*) were made by Johann Bernhard Fischer von Erlach in 1695. It was only partly built when Maria Theresa's court architect, Nikolaus Pacassi, revamped the design in the 1740s. His long, symmetrical palace is a vast corridor of gilded and crimson displays—Japanese, Italian, Persian and Indian works of art, ceiling frescoes celebrating the Habsburgs and 18th-century furniture and porcelain. The palace looks out on a park with immaculate parterres and hedges and a vista of ornamental pools and fountains.

The park The 18th-century gardens were later partially restyled by Adrian van Steckhoven. On top of the hill is the Gloriette, a piece of pure architecture, originally with no interior (a café has since been installed). It is worth climbing up to it for the view over the city. The zoo has retained its 18th-century plan with a baroque pavilion in the middle, but now includes modern enclosures and buildings. Other additions are a spectacular 19th-century glasshouse and a labyrinth for kids in the restored maze.

THE BASICS

www.schoenbrunn.at

See map ▷ 92

811 13-239

Palace: Apr–Jun, Sep, Oct daily 8.30–5; Jul, Aug 8.30–6; Nov–Mar 8.30–4.30. Carriage Museum: Apr–Oct daily 9–6, Nov–Mar 10–4. Zoo: Apr–Sep daily 9–6.30; Nov–Jan 9–4.30; Feb 9–5; Mar, Oct 9–5.30. Park: daily 6.30–dusk

Cafés and restaurants

U4 to Schönbrunn or Hietzing (for palm house and zoo)

Bus 10A; trams 10, 58 to Schönbrunn

Good

Palace, zoo: expensive; carriage museum: moderate; park: free

Audio guides. Tours can be booked online

HIGHLIGHTS

- Carriage Museum
- Oriental panels, Vieux-Lacque Room
- Mirrors and frescoed ceiling in the Great Gallery
- Park and Gloriette

TIP

- The Roman Ruin, an artistic fake symbolizing the victory of Rome over Carthage, is close to the *schöner Brunn* (the "beautiful spring").

More to See

AUGARTEN

www.augarten.at

Joseph II opened these gardens to the public in 1775. The porcelain factory in the Augarten Palace can be visited. The Augarten is also host to the Vienna Boys' Choir and an annexe of the Belvedere collection, Augarten Contemporary.

G1 Park 6–dusk

Porcelain Museum Obere Augartenstrasse 1A 211 24-200 Mon–Sat 10–6 U2 to Taborstrasse Tram 2 to Taborstrasse/Obere Augartenstrasse Inexpensive

BESTATTUNGSMUSEUM

www.bestattungsmuseum.at

This museum is near the main entrance to the city's Central Cemetery (Zentralfriedhof). Exhibits focus on Viennese funeral and burial practices using photographs and objects, as well as interactive video presentations.

See map ▷ 93 Wiener Zentralfriedhof Tor 2, Simmeringer Hauptstrasse 234 760 67 Mon–Fri 9–4.30 Trams 6, 71 to Zentralfriedhof (Haupttor) Moderate

Augarten

GÄNSEHÄUFEL

www.gaensehaeufel.at

This is the Lido of Vienna, an island in the Alte Donau (Old Danube), the now dead arm of the river. Facilities include an open-air pool with artificial waves and a water-chute, tennis, minigolf and even a place where rock climbers can try their skills. Extremely crowded on hot summer days.

See map ▷ 93 Moissigasse 21 269 90 16 May–Sep Mon–Fri 9–8, Sat–Sun 8–8 U1 to Kaisermühlen VIC (Vienna International Centre), then bus 92A to Schüttauplatz or occasional shuttle services Good Moderate

KIRCHE AM STEINHOF

The weird and wonderful Steinhof Church was built by Otto Wagner for patients with mental illnesses in 1907. The interior is clinically white with special fittings, full of wonders from Secession artists—most notably Kolo Moser's glass-mosaic windows.

See map ▷ 92 Sozialmedizinisches Zentrum, Baumgartner Höhe 1 910 60-11007 Sat 4pm–5pm, Sun 12–4 (open access). Guided tour in German Sat 3pm, Sun 4pm or by prior arrangement Buses 47A, 48A to Psychiatrisches Zentrum None Tours inexpensive for groups of 10 people or more; expensive for smaller groups and tours in English

TECHNISCHES MUSEUM

www.technischesmuseum.at

Here you can explore the inventions and technical development of Austria past and present. The

museum displays its items in user-friendly and spacious settings.

See map ▷ 92 Mariahilferstrasse 212 89998-0 Mon–Fri 9–6, Sat–Sun, hols 10–6. Closed 1 Jan, 1 May, 1 Nov, 25, 31 Dec Café Trams 52, 58 from U3 Westbahnhof to Penzinger Strasse Good Moderate

WIENER STRASSENBAHNMUSEUM

www.wiener-tramwaymuseum.org

Noteworthy in the Tramway Museum are the horse- and steam-driven trams of the 19th century and a New York streetcar. Vintage tram carriages can be hired for special occasions.

L7 Ludwig-Kössler-Platz 7909-41800 May–early Oct Sat–Sun, hols 10–5 U3 to Schlachthausgasse Bus 77A to Ludwig-Kössler-Platz; tram 18 to Schlachthausgasse Moderate

WITTGENSTEIN HAUS

www.haus-wittgenstein.at

Ludwig Wittgenstein, one of the most famous philosophers of the 20th century, designed this austere house for his sister in the 1920s. The house reflects its creator's intellect; built in the Bauhaus style, it is curious rather than architecturally appealing. It is now owned by the government of Bulgaria and is used as the Bulgarian Cultural Institute.

J5 Parkgasse 18 713 3164 Mon–Thu 10–5 U3 to Rochusgasse Free Accessible for functions of the Bulgarian Cultural Institute

WOTRUBA KIRCHE

www.georgenberg.at

This extraordinary modern church, designed by the sculptor Fritz Wotruba and constructed in 1976, seems to have been assembled with randomly jumbled concrete blocks and lit by arbitrarily placed narrow glass panels.

See map ▷ 92 Georgsgasse/Rysergasse (Mauer, 23rd District) 888 61 47. Guided tours 650 332 4833 Sat and before church hols 2pm–8pm, Sun 9–5 Tram 60 to Maurer Hauptplatz, then bus 60A to Kaserngasse

Wotruba Kirche

Excursions

THE BASICS

www.baden.at
Distance: 25km (16 miles)
Journey Time: 1 hour
Tourist Office: 02252/ 22 600-600
Badner Bahn (blue-white tram) from Oper. Supplementary fare from Vienna's city border
Operetta performances in the Stadttheater end Jun to mid-Sep

BADEN

A geological fault where the eastern edge of the Alps meets the Vienna Basin is responsible for the mineral springs at Baden, first exploited by the Romans. The now-sleepy town became a fashionable spa during the Biedermeier period (1815–48).

In the early 19th century, the Habsburg court under Emperor Franz I used Baden as its imperial summer residence. Mozart wrote his sublime *Ave Verum* chorus for the choir of the parish church. The town is full of Joseph Kornhäusel's neoclassical architecture. Both a tram (*Lokalbahn*) and bus service run from Oper to Baden (25km/16 miles).

THE BASICS

www.bratislava.sk
Distance: 70km (43 miles)
Journey Time: 1 hour
From Wien Hauptbahnhof to Bratislava Hlavná stanica (Main Station) or Petrzalka twice every hour
Twin City Liner
(▷ 94)

BRATISLAVA

For 1,000 years a part of Hungary and for more than two centuries its capital, Bratislava became the capital of the newly independent Slovak Republic in 1993.

While the old city core has preserved its medieval and baroque charm, the outskirts of Bratislava have boomed since the fall of the Iron Curtain in 1989. A highlight is St. Martin's Cathedral, where 11 kings of Hungary were crowned. The views over the city from either the castle terraces or the tower of the Novy most (New Bridge) are spectacular.

THE BASICS

www.stift-heiligenkreuz.org
Distance: 35km (22 miles)
Journey Time: 1 hour
02258-8703-0
From Wien Hauptbahnfhof (U1) or Wien Meidling (U6) to Mödling, then bus 365
Mon–Sat at 10, 11, 2, 3, 4. Sun, hols no tour at 10
Moderate

HEILIGENKREUZ

This abbey, whose name "Holy Cross" is derived from the fragment of the True Cross preserved in a tabernacle on the main altar, was founded in 1133 by the Cistercians.

The beautiful medieval church has a lovely Romanesque nave and Gothic cloister. The cloister dates from the mid-13th century and, as such, marks the transition from Romanesque to early Gothic architecture. Later baroque features include the Trinity Column and St. Joseph Fountain in the courtyard, by Giovanni Giuliani (1664–1744). Visits are by guided tour only, which must be arranged in advance. It's also possible to stay the night as a guest.

KLOSTERNEUBURG

Legend has it that this monastery was founded on the spot where Margrave Leopold III discovered the veil of his wife Agnes after the wind had blown it away when they were out hunting.

The small winegrowers' town upstream from the capital was the residence of the Babenbergs in the 12th century, before they moved to Vienna. In the 18th century, Charles VI planned to turn it into an Austrian Escorial. The Verdun altar with its gilded copper plates from 1181 and the "Archduke's hat," the modest crown of the Duchy of Austria, are the most interesting exhibits. Another attraction in the town is the private Essl Collection of contemporary art (An der Donau-Au 1, tel 02243-370 50-150, Tue–Sun 10–6, Wed until 9, moderate, Wed 5–9pm free).

THE BASICS

www.stift-klosterneuburg.at

Distance: 10km (6 miles)

Journey Time: 20 min by train or bus

☎ 02243-411-0

🚌 Bus 238, 239 from Heiligenstadt to Klosterneuburg-Kierling

🚆 From Spittelau (U4, U6) to Klosterneuburg-Kierling

Monastery

🕐 Daily 9–6. Closed 25, 26 Dec; 24, 31 Dec from 12; 1 Jan from 1

✋ Moderate

LAXENBURG

The former imperial summer resort at Laxenburg has three palaces to visit and an extensive English park.

You come first to the baroque Blue Court (which is not blue at all). Inside the park, to the right, is the Old Palace, and to your left the 19th-century neo-Gothic folly known as the Franzensburg. The latter boasts a fake medieval dungeon, complete with a knight in chains and realistic groans in the background. It is located on an island reached by a cable ferry, or via a bridge from the rear of the park. You can also take a rowboat and discover the hidden beauties of the lake, including a vast romantic grotto.

The Old Palace now houses the Austrian Film Archive, while the Blue Court is the seat of the IIASA, the International Institute for Applied Systems Analysis. In the lavish surroundings of a former imperial pleasure ground, experts ponder the problems of today's environmental, economic and social changes. In early June the grounds and palaces are home to the annual Laxenburg Spring Festival, which features opera, modern music and music theater.

THE BASICS

www.laxenburg.at

www.schloss-laxenburg.at

Distance: 25km (16 miles)

Journey Time: 30 min

🚌 Bus 566 from U1 Wien Hauptbahnhof, hourly

☎ 02236-71226

🕐 Park: daily dawn–dusk. Franzensburg: Easter–Oct daily 11, 2, 3

✋ Park, ferry, Franzensburg tour: inexpensive. Panorama train: moderate

THE BASICS

www.ddsg-blue-danube.at
Distance: 85km (53 miles)
Journey Time: 1.5 hours by train to Melk or Krems
From Westbahnhof (U3, U6) or Franz-Josefs-Bahnhof (trams D, 5)
Heurigen Express (▷ 96)
Cruises: mid-Apr to 26 Oct. Reserve in advance

MELK AND THE WACHAU VALLEY

The huge baroque monastery at Melk commands the entrance to the Wachau Valley on the Danube.

You can take a cruise either from Melk downstream to Krems in the Wachau or from Krems upstream to Melk. Stroll through the narrow streets of Krems or see an art exhibition in the Kunsthalle. The river valley, which is a UNESCO World Heritage Site, is adorned with vineyards, picturesque villages and medieval castle ruins such as Dürnstein, where the English King Richard the Lionheart was held prisoner from 1192 to 1193.

THE BASICS

www.seegrotte.at
Distance: 20km (13 miles)
Journey Time: 1 hour
02236-26364
Apr–Oct daily 9–5; Nov–Mar Mon–Fri 9–3, Sat–Sun, hols 9–3.30
Schnellbahn to Mödling then buses 364 or 365

SEEGROTTE HINTERBRÜHL

Situated in a former gypsum mine, this is Europe's biggest underground lake.

Water accumulated in it after an accident during a blasting operation in 1912, and has to be pumped out daily (there are seven sources but no outflow). During World War II, the grotto was taken over by the German military and used to house an underground aircraft factory because of the protection the cave afforded against frequent Allied bombing raids. Nowadays, the grotto is a popular attraction, with visitors cruising the waters in small boats.

THE BASICS

www.semmering.at
www.semmeringbahn.at
Distance: 100km (66 miles)
Journey Time: 2 hours
From Meidling approx. every hour; few are direct

SEMMERING

Completed in 1854, the Semmering railway, which runs southwest from Vienna to the Italian border, was the first mountain railway on the continent.

It is still admired for its sophisticated engineering in a mountainous landscape. In the early 20th century Semmering was a summer retreat for the well-to-do from Vienna and Budapest and Semmering station still exudes a resort atmosphere. In 1998, Semmering Railway was added to the UNESCO World Heritage list. Every few years, the World Cup downhill ski races take place on the Hirschenkogel at the top of the Semmering pass.

Shopping

HUNDERTWASSER VILLAGE
www.hundertwasser-village.com
Colorful prints and other items relating to the artist and architect (▷ 95).
J4 ✉ Kegelgasse 37–39 ☎ 710 41 16 Daily 9–6 Tram 1 to Hetzgasse

MANNER FACTORY OUTLET
Locally produced Neopolitan wafers sold in attractive gift packs, plus Ildefonso chocolates at a small shop attached to the Manner Factory.
Off map at A3 ✉ Wilhelminestrasse 6 ☎ 488 22-3770 Mon–Fri 9–5 Tram 44 to Wilhelminenstrasse

ROCK-SHOP
www.rock-shop.at
A paradise for vinyl collectors. Oldies from the 1950s to the 1970s, mostly singles hits.
H1 ✉ Taborstrasse 70 ☎ 216 89 93 Mon–Fri 9–12, 2–6, Sat 9–12 Tram 2 to Heinestrasse

COSTLY LEATHER

Fashion items such as leather goods are expensive in Vienna. The best selections and prices are found at chain stores like Humanic, in the shopping mall on the southern outskirts of the city (✉ Shopping City Süd, Vösendorf Ikea bus from the Oper).

WIENER PORZELLANFABRIK
www.augarten.at
You can buy Augarten porcelain direct from the factory. Seconds sell at a 20 percent discount.
G1 ✉ Wiener Porzellanmanufaktur, Obere Augartenstrasse 1A ☎ 211 24-200 Mon–Fri 10–6 Tram 2 to Obere Augartenstrasse

Entertainment and Nightlife

ARENA
www.arenavie.com
A music and arts venue.
M8/9 ✉ Baumgasse 80 ☎ 798 85 95 May–Sep daily from 1pm (4pm in winter) U3 to Erdberg

CITY & COUNTRY GOLF CLUB AM WIENERBERG
www.cityandcountry.at
In southern Vienna.
Off map at E9 ✉ Gutheil Schoder-Gasse 7 ☎ 661 23 Bus 16A, 65A to Gutheil Schoder-Gasse

FRITZ EPPEL
www.eppel-boote.at
Boats for rental.
Off map at L1 ✉ Wagramer Strasse 48A ☎ 263 3530 U1 to Alte Donau

SCHÖNBRUNNER SCHLOSSTHEATER
www.kammeroper-schoenbrunn.at
Music students perform lighter opera and operettas in July and August.
Off map at A9 ✉ Schloss Schönbrunn ☎ 664 1111 600 U4 to Schönbrunn

U4
www.u-4.at
An enduring dance club. Live music and theme nights. Nextdoor is a bar.
Off map at A9 ✉ Schönbrunner Strasse 222–228 ☎ 817 11 92-0 Mon–Tue, Thu–Sat 10pm–5am U4 to Meidlinger Hauptstrasse

WIENER STADTHALLE
www.stadthalle.com
Sports complex with an ice rink and Olympic-size pool. Stages concerts, shows and exhibitions.
A5/6 ✉ Vogelweidplatz 14 ☎ 79 999 79 Mon–Fri 1.30–5, Sat–Sun, hols 8–12, 1–5 U6 to Burggasse Tram 18 to Burggasse/Stadthalle

Restaurants

PRICES

Prices are approximate, based on a 3-course meal for one person.
€€€ over €40
€€ €20–€40
€ under €20

DOMMAYER (€€)

www.oberlaa-wien.at

Close to Schönbrunn and the zoo, and revived under the new owners (Oberlaa Konditorei), this is Vienna's oldest music café. Once a month, the female ensemble Wiener Walzmädchen gives a performance. Johann Strauss once played here.

Off map at A9
Auhofstrasse 2 (Hietzing)
877 54 65-0 Daily 7am–10pm Tram 58 to Dommayergasse

DONAUTURM (€€€)

www.donauturm.at

Dine in the revolving restaurant at the top of the Danube Tower. The kitchen specializes in traditional Austrian dishes. Reservations are required.

Off map at L1
Donauturmstrasse 4
263 35 72 Daily 11–3, 6–12; observation deck: 10am–midnight Bus 20B from U1 Kaisermühlen VIC to Donauturm (watch for direction)

FUHRGASSL-HUBER (€€)

www.fuhrgassl-huber.at

One of the most congenial taverns in Neustift's long main street offers a warm welcome. The same family also runs an excellent pension close by.

Off map at D1
Neustift am Walde 68
440 14 05 Mon–Sat 2pm–midnight, Sun, hols 12–12 U4, U6 to Spittelau then bus 35A to Neustift am Walde

MAYER AM PFARRPLATZ (€€)

www.pfarrplatz.at

The most famous *Heuriger* in Heiligenstadt. Beethoven worked on his Ninth Symphony in the house; there's music from 7pm.

Off map at D1
Heiligenstädter Pfarrplatz 2
370 12 87 Daily 4pm–midnight. Closed Christmas to mid-Jan U4 to Heiligenstadt then bus 38A to Fernsprechamt/Pfarrplatz

HEURIGEN

A *Heuriger* is a tavern in its own vineyard, traditionally selling only the current year's *Heuer* (wine). When open, a *Heuriger* is *ausg'steckt*, indicated by a bunch of fir twigs hung outside the door. The basic wine is *Gemischter Satz*, a white blend of local grapes. Roast meats, cheeses and salads are served in most *Heurigen*. The warm atmosphere is quintessentially Viennese, with *Schrammelmusik* playing.

PLACHUTTA (€€€)

www.plachutta.at

If you want to sample the famous *Wiener Tafelspitz* (boiled beef) at its most luxurious, as well as other beef specialties, this is the place. The restaurant is in the suburb of Hietzing, close to Schönbrunn, with another outlet in the Innere Stadt at Wollzeile 38.

Off map at A9
Auhofstrasse 1 877 70 87 Daily 11.30–3, 6–11.30. Closed mid-Jul to mid-Aug U4 to Hietzing Tram 58 to Dommayergasse

WILD (€€)

www.gasthaus-wild.at

Characterful restaurant offering excellent traditional Austrian food and friendly service. Its large terrace is in the shadow of a rail bridge, but you don't notice it.

J4 Radetzkyplatz 1
9209 477 Daily 10am–1am Tram 1 to Radetzkyplatz

ZIMMERMANN (€€)

www.zimmermanns.at

A quiet *Heuriger* off the beaten track and close to the Beethoven House, where the composer's Heiligenstadt Testament letter was written (▷ 96).

Off map at D1
Armbrustergasse 5
370 22 11 Mon–Sat 5pm–midnight, Sun 4pm–11pm U4 to Heiligenstadt then bus 38A to Armbrustergasse

In Vienna there is an extremely broad choice of hotels, and many succeed in combining old-fashioned charm with modern comfort.

Introduction

In Vienna tourist accommodations range from luxury hotels in baroque palaces to much smaller, friendly establishments with a local character, some family run.

Tradition

At the crossroads of Central Europe, Vienna has a long tradition of welcoming guests, from medieval crusaders and merchants to the high-ranking diplomats, officials of international bodies and tourists of today. The names of some hotels—such as Ambassador, König von Ungarn (King of Hungary), Das Triest or Imperial—reflect the city's ancient geographical and historical significance. To stay in one of these is to be transported back in time. These traditional hotels have nevertheless been tastefully modernized, so they fully meet the demands of today's traveler.

Millionaires and Expense Accounts

Vienna has become a top venue for international conferences and is one of the three bases of the UN. The OPEC headquarters are located here and the city attracts well-to-do and influential visitors from Arab nations. The new millionaires from the post-Communist countries of Eastern Europe, plus many of their compatriots, have also become regular visitors. To cater to this new clientele, recent hotel development has been in the mid-range and luxury categories. Nevertheless there are plenty of budget hotels and hostels.

HOTEL LOCATIONS

Most of the famous hotels are inside or on the Ringstrasse. This includes traditional 19th-century luxury hotels like Sacher, Imperial or Bristol, but also newcomers like the Marriot and Le Meridien. Hotels outside the Ringstrasse are less formal and often located on attractive smaller streets or courtyards. Hotels on the outskirts of the city may offer a more parklike environment or gardens, as well as lower prices. Student hostels are mostly in the Inner Districts between the Ringstrasse and Gürtel (Ring Road).

Viennese hotels: Kaiserin Elisabeth; views of Hotel Imperial; Hotel Sacher (top to bottom)

Budget Hotels

PRICES

Expect to pay under €110 for a double room per night in a budget hotel.

DO STEP INN

www.dostepinn.at

This pleasant hotel offers a good location next to the Westbahnhof (West train station), as well as decent shopping and eating on Mariahilfer Strasse. It has a range of modest but clean singles, doubles and suites. There is an adjacent hostel.

A6 Felberstrasse 20 982 33 14 U3, U6 to Westbahnhof

KUGEL

www.hotelkugel.at

Over a century old, and extremely good value near the lively Spittelberg area, which is full of open-air restaurants.

C5/6 Siebensterngasse 43/Neubaugasse 46 523 33 55 Closed early Jan–early Feb U3 to Neubaugasse Bus 13A; tram 49 to Neubaugasse/ Westbahnhofstrasse

LEHRERHAUS

www.hotel-lehrerhaus.at

Run by the Association for Teachers' Accommodation, this pension in the suburb of the Josefstadt sits just behind the Parliament and Rathaus. It has 40 rooms (33 en suite). Vienna's English Theatre is based in the same building.

D4 Lange Gasse 20–22 Josefsgasse 403 23 58 U2 to Rathaus Tram 2 to Rathaus

MARIAHILF HOTEL-PENSION

www.mariahilf-hotel.at

As inexpensive as you'll find in this location near the MuseumsQuartier, this pension has clean, airy rooms sleeping between two and six people. Breakfast room, but no restaurant.

D6 Mariahilferstrasse 49 586 17 81 U3 to Neubaugasse

PENSION WILD

www.pension-wild.com

Traditionally one of the city's cheaper guest-houses, Pension Wild nevertheless offers an excellent location near the center in Josefstadt, with good public transportation links and comfortable rooms in a historic town house. The cheapest rooms come without en suite baths, though sinks with hot and cold water are available in every room.

D4 Lange Gasse 10 406 51 74 U3 to Volkstheater

IN SEARCH OF GOOD VALUE

Other than youth hostels, there are few inexpensive accommodations in Vienna. At the same time, there are still hotels with less than friendly service that charge the (high) going rate. The Viennese themselves remark darkly that the world of hotels is under the eternal sway of the mythical "King Nepp" (from *neppen*, meaning to overcharge). Few escape his tyrannous rule, but there are several (some listed here) that try hard to offer value for money and friendly service.

PRIVATE ROOMS

www.netland.at/wien/apartment-vienna.htm

The website of the official Apartment & Vacation Rental Owner Organization of Vienna helps you book one of the 250 Vienna apartments, vacation rentals and bed-and-breakfasts in all districts of the city.

TIME OUT CITY HOTEL

www.timeout.co.at

This modest bed-and-breakfast, within easy walking distance of the MuseumsQuartier, combines the best of a family-run atmosphere with a location in a historic Jugendstil (Secession) building. The public areas have been given a bright, modern makeover, though the decor in the rooms is more subdued.

D5 Windmuehlgasse 6 587 71 55 U3 to Neubaugasse

Mid-Range Hotels

PRICES

Expect to pay between €110 and €218 per night for a double room in a mid-range hotel.

25HOURS HOTEL VIENNA

www.25hours-hotel.com

The theme at this hotel is the theater and circus, and the rooms have been given a colorful retro makeover. The restaurant serves imaginative Mediterranean cuisine in an eye-catching, post-modern space.

D5 Lerchenfelder Strasse 1–3 521 51-0 U2 to Volkstheater

ALMA BOUTIQUE HOTEL

www.hotel-alma.com

New, family-run design hotel in the Innere Stadt with just 26 rooms.

G4 Hafnersteig 7 533 29 61-0 U1, U4 to Schwedenplatz

ALTSTADT VIENNA

www.altstadt.at

The beautifully furnished upper floors of this late 19th-century house are an informal, friendly breakfast-only hotel.

C5 Kirchengasse 41 522 66 66 U2, U3 to Volkstheater Bus 48A to Kellermanngasse

ALTWIENERHOF

www.altwienerhof.at

Bargain rates, in view of the fine restaurant. The 23 rooms have an opulent Belle Époque look and there is a lovely courtyard.

A8 Herklotzgasse 6 892 60 00 U6 to Gumpendorfer Strasse Bus 57A; trams 6, 18 to Gumpendorfer Strasse

AMADEUS

www.hotel-amadeus.at

A small, but distinguished bed-and-breakfast. The building was once the meeting place for musicians like Brahms and Schubert.

F4 Wildpretmarkt 5 533 8738 U1, U3 to Stephansplatz

BEST WESTERN PREMIER SCHLOSS-HOTEL RÖMISCHER KAISER

www.bestwestern.com

A modest baroque palace in the old city. Delightful—all crimson fabrics and chandeliers. 24 rooms.

F5 Annagasse 16 512 77 51-0 U1, U3 to Stephansplatz

DAY AND NIGHT

The Viennese tend to get up early, but this works to the tourist's advantage, as public transport will be much more comfortable when you are heading for your first sight. By the same token, many Viennese go relatively early to bed and lots of restaurants serve supper quite early. For night owls there are plenty of bars and a good network of nightlong transport.

DAS CAPRI

www.dascapri.at

This medium-size hotel in Leopoldstadt (across the Danube canal from the center) has big modern rooms, some with balconies; gleaming baths; a great breakfast buffet; and a U-Bahn station just outside the front door to take you to the center in around five minutes.

H3 Praterstrasse 44–46 214 84 04 U1 to Nestroyplatz

FLEMINGS HOTEL WIEN-WESTBAHNHOF

www.flemings-hotels.com

A four-star hotel with elegant rooms furnished in a contemporary style, that make a central feature of their glass-and-granite shower cubicles. Brasserie and wine bar.

B6 Neubaugürtel 26–28 227 37-0 U3 to Westbahnhof, U6 to Burggasse Trams 5 to Burggasse, 18 to Westbahnhof

HOLLMANN BELETAGE HOTEL

www.hollmann-beletage.at

Designed to feel like a cutting-edge residential apartment, where guests are encouraged to relax as if they are at home. The six-course breakfast menu changes daily. The nearby Hollmann Salon (▷ 45) restaurant is innovative too.

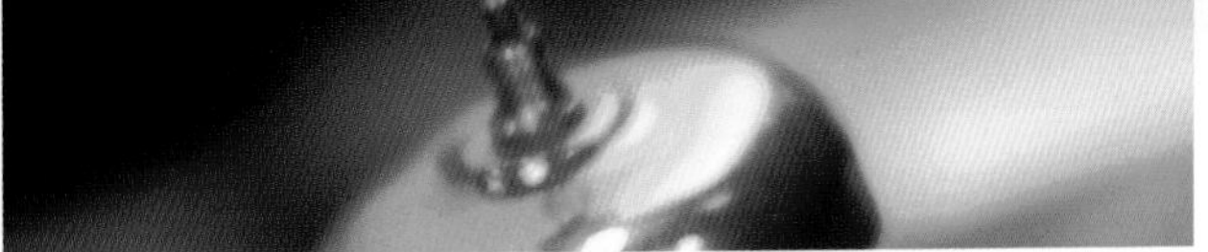

G4 Köllnerhofgasse 6 96 11 960 U1, U4 to Schwedenplatz Trams 1, 2 to Schwedenplatz

HOTEL-PENSION MUSEUM

www.hotelmuseum.at

Art lovers and academics are attracted to this old-fashioned pension with 15 large rooms.

D5 Museumstrasse 3 523 44 26 U2, U3 to Volkstheater

HOTEL RATHAUS WINE AND DESIGN

www.hotel-rathaus-wien.at

Each double room is dedicated to a different Austrian winemaker, and the staff will discuss the merits of different wines in the wine lounge. Excellent breakfast.

D4 Lange Gasse 13 400 11 22 U2 to Rathaus/Volkstheater, U3 to Volkstheater

HOTEL WANDL

www.hotel-wandl.com

Family-run hotel, next to Peterskirche in a partly 12th-century building.

F4 Petersplatz 9 534 55-0 U1, U3 to Stephansplatz

KAISERIN ELISABETH

www.kaiserinelisabeth.at

This 63-room hotel has a whiff of imperial nostalgia. A good choice if you want to be immersed in the Altstadt atmosphere.

F4 Weihburggasse 3 515 26-0 U1, U3 to Stephansplatz

KÖNIG VON UNGARN

www.kvu.at

An 18th-century building next to the Figarohaus. Rooms ring an airy, glassed-in courtyard. Prestigious restaurant. 33 rooms.

G4 Schulerstrasse 10 515 84-0 U1, U3 to Stephansplatz

LANDHAUS FUHRGASSL-HUBER

www.fuhrgassl-huber.at

Located in a wine village by the Vienna Woods. With its peasant-style furniture and a summer courtyard, this one is special. 38 rooms.

Off map at D1 Rathstrasse 24, Neustift am Walde 440 30 33 Bus 35A to Neustift am Walde

PENSION NOSSEK

www.pension-nossek.at

Good location in the heart of the city; the pedestrianized area ensures quiet. The 30 rooms range from spacious to compact. Pleasant service. Reserve well in advance.

F4 Graben 17 533 70 41-0 U1, U3 to Stephansplatz

SUBURBS

While luxury hotels are clearly concentrated in the Inner City or Ringstrassen area, many mid-range ones are in the suburbs. Access to the city center is not a problem, as most of them are near U-Bahn or tram stations. They will also seduce you into exploring quite charming areas not otherwise visited.

PERTSCHY PALAIS HOTEL

www.pertschy.com

Set in a baroque mansion, this pension is just off the Graben. The 55 rooms are spacious, with period furniture.

F4 Habsburgergasse 5 534 49-0 U1, U3 to Stephansplatz

STEIGENBERGER HOTEL HERRENHOF

www.herrenhof-wien.steigenberger.at

This sleek, contemporary hotel is close to the Hofburg. Its restaurant serves good modern Viennese cuisine, and there's an atmospheric piano bar and café. It's at the top end of the mid-range bracket.

E4 Herrengasse 10 53404-0 U3 to Herrengasse

ZIPSER

www.zipser.at

The Zipser is a premium address for cultural tourists who also want to enjoy the special flair of Vienna's smartest suburb, Josefstadt. The area has a pleasant villagey and funky atmosphere.

C3 Lange Gasse 49 404 54-0 U2 to Rathaus

Luxury Hotels

PRICES

Expect to pay over €218 per night for a double room at a luxury hotel.

BRISTOL

www.bristolvienna.com

Old-fashioned elegance on the Ringstrasse. A recent refurbishment has given the rooms an overdue update. Some rooms have evocative views over the Opera.

F5 Kärntner Ring 1 515 16-0 U1, U2, U4 to Karlsplatz/Oper

DO & CO HOTEL VIENNA

www.doco.com

There's a Turkish influence in the sumptuous styling of the 43 rooms, and some interesting extras—including a TV in the bathroom, and both three- and two-pin plug sockets. The superb Do & Co restaurant (▷ 44) is on the seventh floor.

F4 Stephansplatz 12 24 188 U1, U3 to Stephansplatz

GRAND HOTEL WIEN

www.grandhotelwien.com

This Imperial-style hotel is one of the city's classics. Its celebrity guests range from Johann Strauss to Paul McCartney. Its top-class restaurants include Le Ciel (▷ 43) and Unkai.

F5 Kärntner Ring 9 515 80-0 U1, U2, U4 to Karlsplatz/Oper Trams 1, 2, D to Opernring

HOTEL IMPERIAL

www.imperialvienna.com

This former palace is also the official State Hotel where visiting dignitaries stay.

F6 Kärntner Ring 16 501 10-0 U1, U2, U4 to Karlsplatz Trams 2, D to Schwarzenbergplatz

HOTEL SACHER

www.sacher.com

Vienna's most celebrated hotel. The 152 rooms are opulent and classically furnished.

F5 Philharmonikerstrasse 4 514 56-555 U1, U2, U4 to Karlsplatz/Oper

PALAIS HANSEN KEMPINSKI VIENNA

www.kempinski.com/wien

This hotel occupies an imposing 19th-century palace. Amenities include two restaurants, a cigar lounge and a Turkish-style spa. Rooms are high-end contemporary in look.

F3 Schottenring 24 236 10 00 U2, U4 to Schottenring

HOTEL SACHER

Sacher was once famous for its *chambres séparées*, where aristocrats "entertained" dancers. It was founded in 1876 by the son of the cook to Prince Metternich and carried on by his widow, Anna, who ruled her hotel with an iron rod. Just after World War I, she single-handedly held off a mob of rioting workers, but she also had a strong social conscience and fed the poor from the kitchen.

RADISSON BLU STYLE HOTEL

www.radissonblu.com

This high-end hotel offers sharp and colorful contemporary design in the rooms, as well as flat-screen TVs. The inhouse Sapori Restaurant has a modern take on traditional Austrian cooking.

E4 Herrengasse 12 227 80-0 U3 to Herrengasse

THE RING

www.theringhotel.com

This classy, modern hotel is in a historic building. With just 68 rooms, it has a boutique feel. There is a spa and its restaurant—At Eight (▷ 43)—is award winning.

F6 Kärntner Ring 8 22 1 22 U1, U2, U4 to Karlsplatz/Oper Trams 1, 2, D to Opernring

SOFITEL VIENNA STEPHANSDOM

www.sofitel.com

This relatively recent entry to the luxury category sits in the up-and-coming 2nd District, and has a striking design in glass and steel. There are panoramic views from the top-floor Le Loft restaurant and bar.

G3 Praterstrasse 1 906 160 U3 to Schwedenplatz

This section supplies you with all the practical information needed to make your stay in Vienna as comfortable as possible, including tips for using public transportation, when to go and money matters.

Planning Ahead

When to Go

Most of the important festivals and events are held in spring and summer. The main opera and concert seasons kick off in autumn. Some prime attractions (such as the Lipizzaners and the Vienna Boys' Choir) take a summer break and may be on tour some months.

TIME

Vienna is one hour ahead of the UK, six hours ahead of New York and nine hours ahead of Los Angeles.

AVERAGE DAILY MAXIMUM TEMPERATURES

JAN	FEB	MAR	APR	MAY	JUN	JUL	AUG	SEP	OCT	NOV	DEC
34°F	37°F	48°F	59°F	66°F	73°F	79°F	77°F	68°F	59°F	45°F	39°F
1°C	3°C	9°C	15°C	19°C	23°C	26°C	25°C	20°C	15°C	7°C	4°C

Spring (March to May) is rainy and sometimes fairly cool until mid-April.
Summer (June to August) seems to be getting hotter every year!
Autumn (September to October) is the most pleasant time to visit, when it is not too hot and mostly dry.
Winter (November to February) can be bitterly cold, often with heavy snow from late December.
If you suffer from migraines or circulation problems you may be affected by the *Föhn* wind blowing off the Alps.

WHAT'S ON

February *Opernball* (Opera Ball): The highlight of the social calendar.
March–April *OsterKlang*: Sacred music for Easter in St. Stephen's, the Musikverein and elsewhere.
February–June and September–December *Equestrian ballet*: Lipizzaner shows at the Hofburg.
April *Frühlingsfestival* (Mar/Apr to early May): Concerts in the Musikverein and Konzerthaus.
May *Maifest* (1 May): Celebrations mostly in the Prater.
Wiener Festwochen (May to mid-Jun): Arts festival in the MuseumsQuartier and other venues.
June *Open-air festival* (end Jun): Pop music on the Danube Island.
July *Jazz Fest Wien* (Jun–Jul): At the Opera House and various jazz clubs.
Operimsommer (Jul–Aug): Classical concerts and operas at the Theater an der Wien.
Music on Film (Jul–Sep): Films (mostly opera) on a screen before the Rathaus.
Summer Operetta (Jul–Aug): Schönbrunner Schlosstheater.
October *Viennale*: Film Festival.
Vienna Design Week: International design festival at various locations.
November *Wien Modern* (end Oct–Nov): One of Europe's biggest festivals of contemporary music.
November–December *Christkindlmarkt* (mid-Nov to 24 Dec): A Christmas fair in front of the Rathaus.
New Year's Eve *Silvesterpfad:* Shows and concerts.
Die Fledermaus: At the State Opera.

Vienna Online

www.austria.info
An easy-to-navigate site with information on all types of holiday in Austria, including car, motorcycle and hiking itineraries. Other features include a listing of events, weather forecasts, water temperatures in the lakes, plus webcam pictures of towns, landscapes and buildings.

www.wien.gv.at
This site offers diverse general information on the city, from politics and culture to urban development and the environment. Detailed map showing building numbers, one-way streets and City Bike stations (▷ 119).

www.vienna.info
Official site of the Vienna Tourist Board with information on sightseeing, eating out, culture and more. Useful for locating theater booking offices and (in some cases) booking online. The 72-hour itinerary is a good tour for first-time visitors and those with limited time.

www.aboutvienna.org
Alongside general information on the city, this English-language site offers focused sections on Viennese culture, cuisine, etiquette and the German language, as well as tips for those living and working in the city.

www.falter.at
Website for the weekly paper *Der Falter*, the city's best online resource for finding out what's happening around town. Dedicated sections on new movies, festivals, parties and events. In German only, but easy to navigate.

www.viennaconcerts.com
This website provides details of upcoming concert programs, and allows you to reserve tickets at the Staatsoper (State Opera) and other music venues in the city. There are packages available, and also a link to accommodations options.

TRAVEL SITES

www.fodors.com
A complete travel-planning site. Research prices and weather; book air tickets, cars and rooms; pose questions to fellow visitors; and find links to other sites.

www.oeamtc.at
Invaluable for motorists, this site (only in German) informs about the current state of traffic on Austrian roads, roadworks, weather conditions and much more. The visuals will help non-German speakers.

www.wienerlinien.at
The official website of the Wiener Linien, Vienna's public transportation authority. Handy information in English on tickets and fares, as well as a convenient online timetable to help plan journeys around town.

www.tourmycountry.com
Another website in English—although written by an Austrian—that has details on traveling and sightseeing in Austria, and aims to take a personal and opinionated approach.

Getting There

ENTRY REQUIREMENTS

Visitors from the UK, EU countries, the US and Canada need a passport (valid for at least six months) but do not need a visa. For the latest passport and visa information, check the relevant embassy website (Britain: www.bmeia.gv.at; US: www.austria.org). Austria is part of the Schengen Zone. This means that there are no border restrictions for travel between countries that are part of the agreement (including adjacent countries Italy, Germany, Hungary, Czech Republic and Slovakia).

VACCINATIONS

Some wooded areas of Austria are home to *Zecken*, a kind of tick whose bite can transmit encephalitis, which in a few cases proves fatal. Enquire at the Austrian consulate about inoculation.

CUSTOMS REGULATIONS

Duty-free limits for non-European Union visitors are: 200 cigarettes or 250g of tobacco or 50 cigars; 4 liters of wine and 1 liter of spirits.

AIRPORT

Vienna International Airport (Flughafen Wien) is 19km (12 miles) east of the city at Schwechat. The airport has extensive shopping facilities, restaurants, bars, newsstands and car-rental desks.

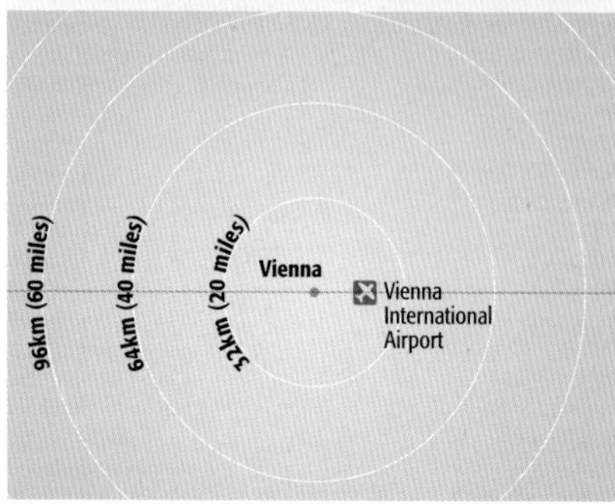

ARRIVING BY AIR

The most convenient option for transportation to the city from Vienna International Airport (tel 7007 22233, www.viennaairport.com) is the Vienna Airport Lines bus (tel 7007-32300) to and from Vienna International Centre, Schwedenplatz and Westbahnhof (20–30 minutes, €8). The CAT express train (www.cityairporttrain.com) to Wien Mitte costs €11 and runs from 5.36am to 11.35pm; journey time 16 minutes. The S-Bahn (Schnellzug) rapid transit service is slower (24 minutes) but cheaper (€4.80) and runs from the Flughafen via Wien Mitte to Floridsdorf. Timetables of the above services are shown on the airport website. Taxis from the airport cost between €35 and €45.

ARRIVING BY TRAIN

Trains are operated by the Austrian Federal Railways (Österreichische Bundesbahn/ÖBB). The ÖBB offers direct connections to many European cities, including Bratislava, Budapest, Munich and Prague. For train information and bookings, visit www.oebb.at or call 05-1717 (24 hours).

Most trains arrive at and depart from one of two stations: Wien Hauptbahnhof (Main Railway Station; Am Hauptbahnhof 1; U1 to Südtiroler Platz/Hauptbahnhof) or Wien Westbahnhof (Western Railway Station; Europaplatz 2; U3, U6 to Westbahnhof). As a rule, most international trains, including from Prague, Bratislava and Budapest, use Wien Hauptbahnhof, while trains from Germany, western Europe and western Austria use Wien Westbahnhof. Be sure to check your ticket carefully to make certain which station your train is using.

ARRIVING BY CAR

Vienna is reached from Germany, Salzburg and Linz via the West Autobahn (A1); from the Italian and Slovenian borders and Graz it is reached via the South Autobahn (A2); from the Hungarian and Slovak borders it is reached via the East Autobahn (A4); and from the Czech border it is reached from Prague via the North Autobahn (A22) and from Brno via the future A5. All motorists are obliged to purchase a windscreen sticker—a *maut pickerl*—at the border, which serves as a general highway toll. A 10-day sticker costs €8.70. Tolls are also payable in most neighboring countries.

ARRIVING BY BUS

International bus lines (www.eurolines.at) arrive at the bus terminal at Erdbergstrasse 200A opposite U3 Erdberg (tel 798 29 00). The S-Bahn leaves from here, along with tram 18.

ARRIVING BY BOAT

June to September, weekly cruise ships run on the Danube between Passau (Germany) and Vienna. May to early October, there is a hydrofoil connection to Budapest three times a week (daily in August). Ships dock at the DDSG (www.ddsg-blue-danube.at) berth near the Reichsbrücke. From late March to mid-October the Twin City Liner hydrofoil (▷ 94) runs several times daily to Bratislava from the ferry station at Schwedenbrücke.

INSURANCE

EU nationals receive reduced-cost medical treatment with the EHIC (European Health Insurance Card)—obtain this before you go. Full health and travel insurance is still advised. US visitors should check their health cover before departure and buy a supplementary policy if necessary.

VISITORS WITH DISABILITIES

Facilities have improved in museums and some other major sights, but access is not always guaranteed. Older trams and buses remain impossible for anyone in a wheelchair, but most U-Bahn stations are now better equipped with escalators and elevators, and tram stops now indicate on their display boards whether the approaching trams have lowered platforms for alighting. The tourist board website (www.vienna.info) gives the detailed status of transportation, hotels, sights, museums and more. The tourist office also publishes a 130-page guide for visitors with disabilities. It is regularly updated, and can be downloaded from the same website.

Getting Around

TAXIS

- Cabs are efficient and not unreasonably expensive by Austrian standards.
- You can order a cab by phone: tel 31 300, 40 100 or 601 60.
- Tips are 10 percent.
- There are supplements for late-night or weekend rides, plus per head and per piece of luggage.
- Taxis ordered by telephone usually arrive in about five minutes in the heart of the city and inner suburbs.

Vienna is covered by an overlapping network of U-Bahnen (underground trains), Strassenbahnen (trams) and buses. Newsagents (*Tabaktrafik*) sell tickets for public transportation. Main U-Bahn and S-Bahn (rapid-transit railway) stations have ticket counters and all have ticket machines. Taxis can be hired at taxi stands in the city and at the larger public transportation terminals. Officially it is not permitted to hail them in the street, but some will stop for you.

INTEGRATED SYSTEM

- Maps and information about the transportation network can be obtained at the Wiener Linien information office at the Karlsplatz end of Opern Passage (tel 790 91 00) or on the website at www.wienerlinien.at.
- Buy tickets for the U-Bahn, Strassenbahn, buses or S-Bahn from newsagents or at the counters in main U-Bahn and S-Bahn stations. An easy one to find is at the Karlsplatz end of the Opern Passage, at the entrance to U1, U2, U4.
- A single journey card must be validated at the entrance to the underground, or on a tram or bus, using the stamping machines. It can be used for one unbroken ride, including changes of line, or changes from S-Bahn/U-Bahn to tram, to bus. Valid one hour from stamping.
- Penalties for riding without a valid ticket are heavy and checks are quite frequent.

TYPES OF TICKET

- Excursion or season tickets are valid on all parts of the network and even on suburban buses (up to the city boundary).
- Individual tickets are much more expensive per ride, and the machines dispensing them on trams are complicated.
- Good-value monthly or weekly tickets allow unlimited travel all over the network for their duration. No photo is required.
- The *8 Tage-Karte* provides a book of 8 strips, each valid for travel all over the network the day it is validated until 1am the following day. If

there are two or more of you, validate one strip per person. Start with strip No. 1.

- You can buy blocks of tickets for single rides, as well as 24-hour and 72-hour time tickets (useful for short-term visitors).
- Time tickets and the *8 Tage-Karte* must be validated at the commencement of the period of use and are then good for the period stipulated.
- *Wien-Karte* is a 48-hour or 72-hour card with discounts on entry charges to many sights.
- Children under six travel free.

U-BAHN

- There are five lines. Oddly there is U1, U2, U3, U4 and U6 but no U5. U2 follows a semicircular route around the Ringstrasse and beyond.
- The U-Bahn maps found on platforms are color-coded and also show connections to other forms of transportation. Note the end-stop of the direction you want; this will be shown on the sign of the appropriate platform.
- Three lines (U1, U2, U4) meet at Karlsplatz/Oper.
- Main stations have lifts and/or escalators.
- You may take bicycles into designated cars on the U-Bahn (except during rush hour) for an additional charge.
- The S-Bahn (*Schnellbahn*) is a rapid-transit railway bringing commuters from the suburbs to the major traffic connections of the city.

TRAMS/BUSES

- The route is clearly marked at the tram stop and on a card inside. Check you are going in the right direction.
- Bus routes fill the gaps between the mostly radial tram lines. Night buses on main routes run every 30 minutes from Schwedenplatz after 12.30am until around 5am. No supplement is payable.
- The small hopper buses (1A, 2A and 3A) have circular routes through the Inner City with stops at or near virtually all places of interest.

SENSIBLE PRECAUTIONS

- Lock valuables in your hotel safe and don't carry large amounts of cash. Crime is low in Vienna, but high-season pickpockets are busy.
- Avoid the main railway stations at night and the red-light district along the Gürtel.

DRIVING

- Avoid taking your car into the districts inside the Gürtel and especially into the old city inside the Ringstrasse, where underground parking is expensive and above-ground parking difficult and complicated.

CITY BIKE CARD

- At around 120 self-service stations you may rent a bike with a City Bike Card at a very low rate (visit www.citybikewien.at for details on how to obtain a card, but note you'll have to enter a valid credit or debit card number).

Essential Facts

EMBASSIES AND CONSULATES

- **Australia** Mattiellistrasse 2–4 506 740
- **Canada** Laurenzerberg 2 5313 830 00
- **Ireland** Rotenturmstrasse 16–18 715 4246
- **New Zealand** Mattiellistrasse 2–4/3 505 30 21
- **UK** Jaurésgasse 12 7161 30
- **US** Boltzmanngasse 16 313 39-0 (embassy) or Parkring 12A 31 339-7535 (consulate)

MONEY

The euro (€) is Austria's official currency. Notes are in denominations of 5, 10, 20, 50, 100, 200 and 500 euros, and coins in 1 and 2 euros and 1, 2, 5, 10, 20 and 50 cents.

ELECTRICITY

- The voltage is 220 volts AC and two-pin plugs are used.

ETIQUETTE

- Titles are important; if you know which one to use (eg *Herr Doktor*), use it. Address the waiter as *Herr Ober*, the waitress as *Fräulein*.

LOST PROPERTY

- Report loss or theft to the nearest police station.
- Lost and Found Office at Bastiengasse 36–38 (tel 4000 8091, open Mon–Fri 8–3, until 5.30pm on Thu).
- Railway Lost Property (tel 930 00-22222).
- Vienna Transport System Lost Property (tel 7909-43 188).

MEDICAL TREATMENT

- Vienna General Hospital (Allgemeines Krankenhaus) is at Währinger Gürtel 18–20 (tel 404 00-0, www.akhwien.at).
- The Barmherzige Brüder (Brothers of Mercy) treat patients free of charge at their hospital on Johannes von Gott Platz 1 (2nd District, tel 211 21-0, www.barmherzige-brueder.at).

MONEY MATTERS

- Credit cards are accepted by most hotels, leading shops and more expensive restaurants.
- Bankomat machines giving cash against international credit or debit cards with PIN numbers are plentiful in the city.

NATIONAL HOLIDAYS

- 1 Jan
- 6 Jan (Epiphany)
- Easter Monday
- 1 May (State Holiday)
- *Christi Himmelfahrt* (Ascension Day)
- Whit Monday
- Corpus Christi (second Thu after Whitsun)
- 15 Aug (Assumption of the Virgin)
- 26 Oct (National Day)

- 1 Nov (All Saints)
- 8 Dec (Conception)
- 24–26 Dec (everything closes from midday on Christmas Eve)

OPENING HOURS

- Shops: Mon–Fri 9–6, Sat 9–5 (food shops may open earlier). Retailers have a choice of whether to open on Saturdays, and many—particularly outside the center—prefer to stay closed or open only until noon. Most shops open 9–6 on the four Saturdays before Christmas.
- Banks: Mon–Fri 8–12.30, 1.30–3; Thu 1.30–5.30. In the city some stay open at lunch.
- Offices: Mon–Fri 8–4, but may close earlier on Friday.

PHARMACIES

- Pharmacies normally open Mon–Fri 8–12, 2–6, Sat 8–12.
- English-speaking pharmacists include Internationale Apotheke (Kärntner Ring 17, tel 512 28 25), Schweden-Apotheke, Pharmacie Internationale (Schwedenplatz 2, tel 533 2911).

POST OFFICES

- There is a general website for the postal system at www.post.at.
- Fleischmarkt 19, tel 0577 677-1010, open Mon–Fri 7am–10pm, Sat–Sun 9am–10pm.
- Westbahnhof, tel 832 61 10, open Mon–Fri 7am–9pm, Sat 9am–6pm, Sun 9am–2pm.

TELEPHONES

- Telephone cards are sold in *Tabaktrafik* shops (newsagents) and at post offices. Some telephones in the Kohlmarkt/Graben area take credit cards.
- To call Vienna from the UK dial 00431. To call the UK from Vienna, dial 0044.
- To call Vienna from the US dial 011431. To call the US from Vienna, dial 001.
- Directory assistance for Austria and the EU is on 118 877; for everywhere else call 0900 11 8877.

EMERGENCY NUMBERS

- European general emergency number ☎ 112
- Ambulance ☎ 144
- Doctor on call ☎ 141
- Fire ☎ 122
- Police ☎ 133
- ÖAMTC (breakdown service equivalent to AA) ☎ 120

TOURIST INFORMATION

- Tourist-Info Wien ☎ 24 555, www.vienna.info

Main Branch
✉ Albertinaplatz (corner of Maysedergasse)
🕒 Daily 9–7

Vienna International Airport
✉ Arrivals Hall 🕒 Daily 7am–10pm

Main Train Station
✉ Am Hauptbahnhof 1
🕒 Daily 9–5

Language

The Austrian variant of *Hochdeutsch* (High German) is marked enough to warrant a small dictionary for German visitors, but will not trouble the foreign tourist who has learned German. *Wienerisch* (the local dialect of the Viennese) is more difficult, but most natives will respond with the *Hochdeutsch* they have learned in school if addressed in this way by a foreigner.

THE BASICS	
ja	yes
nein	no
bitte	please
danke	thank you
bitte schön	you're welcome
Grüss Gott	hello
guten Morgen	good morning
guten Abend	good evening
gute Nacht	good night
auf Wiedersehen	goodbye
Entschuldigen Sie bitte	Excuse me please
Sprechen Sie Englisch?	Do you speak English?
ich verstehe nicht	I don't understand
Wiederholen Sie das, bitte	Please repeat that
Sprechen Sie langsamer bitte	Please speak more slowly
heute	today
gestern	yesterday
morgen	tomorrow
jetzt	now
gut	good
Ich heisse...	My name is...
Wie heissen Sie?	What's your name?
Ich komme aus...	I'm from...
Wie geht es Ihnen?	How are you?
Sehr gut, danke	Fine, thank you
Wie spät ist es?	What is the time?
wo	where
wann	when
warum	why
wer	who

USEFUL WORDS	
klein/gross	small/large
kalt/warm	cold/warm
rechts/links	right/left
geradeaus	straight ahead
nahe/weit	near/far
geschlossen	closed
offen	open

OUT AND ABOUT

Wieviel kostet es?	How much does it cost?
teuer	expensive
billig	inexpensive
Wo sind die Toiletten?	Where are the toilets?
Wo ist die Bank?	Where's the bank?
der Bahnhof	station
der Flughafen	airport
das Postamt	post office
die Apotheke	pharmacy
die Polizei	police
das Krankenhaus	hospital
der Arzt	doctor
Hilfe	help
Haben Sie einen Stadtplan?	Do you have a city map?
Fahren Sie mich bitte zum/zur/nach...	Please take me to...
Ich möchte hier aussteigen	I'd like to get out here
Ich habe mich verlaufen/ verfahren	I am lost
Können Sie mir helfen?	Can you help me?

NUMBERS

eins	1
zwei	2
drei	3
vier	4
fünf	5
sechs	6
sieben	7
acht	8
neun	9
zehn	10
elf	11
zwölf	12
dreizehn	13
zwanzig	20
einundzwanzig	21
dreissig	30
vierzig	40
fünfzig	50
sechzig	60
siebzig	70
achtzig	80
neunzig	90
hundert	100
tausend	1000
million	million

AT THE HOTEL/RESTAURANT

die Speisekarte	menu
das Frühstück	breakfast
das Mittagesen	lunch
das Abendessen	dinner
der Weisswein	white wine
der Rotwein	red wine
das Bier	beer
das Brot	bread
die Milch	milk
der Zucker	sugar
das Wasser	water
die Rechnung	bill (check)
das Zimmer	room
Ich bin allergisch gegen...	I am allergic to...
Ich bin Vegetarier	I am a vegetarian

COLORS

schwarz	black
blau	blue
braun	brown
rot	red
grün	green
weiss	white
gelb	yellow
rosa	pink
orange	orange
grau	grey
lila	purple

Timeline

MUSICAL NOTES

Music has reverberated around Vienna since the days when the *Minnesänger* (poets of chivalry) performed at the Babenberg court in the 13th century. Members of the Habsburg dynasty were patrons of Gluck, Haydn, Mozart and Beethoven, among others.
Key musical dates include:
1782 Mozart's opera *The Abduction from the Seraglio* premieres at the Court Theater.
1792 Beethoven settles in Vienna.
1828 In June, Franz Schubert completes *Die Winterreise* song cycle. He dies 19 November, age 31.
1867 Johann Strauss Junior's *On the Beautiful Blue Danube* is performed by the Vienna Male Choral Society; it flops.
1897 Gustav Mahler becomes director of the Vienna opera, initiating a period of imaginative productions.

5th–1st century BC The Celtic Boier tribe settles on the site of today's Belvedere Palace.

15BC The Romans conquer the area.

AD400–791 The Romans withdraw. Charlemagne creates the *Ostmark* (Eastern Region of his empire).

881 The Salzburg annals recall a battle at *Weniam*—the first reference to the name *Wien* (Vienna).

1156 Austria becomes a Babenberg dukedom and Vienna the ducal residence.

1278 640 years of Habsburg rule begins.

1421 Pogrom against the Viennese Jews. Two hundred are burned alive.

1517 The advent of Lutheranism in Vienna.

1521 The Spanish and German realms of the Habsburgs, ruled by Charles V, are divided. Charles's brother, Ferdinand I, takes Austria.

1529 The first Turkish siege of Vienna.

1551 The Jesuits are invited to the city. The Counter-Reformation begins.

1683 The second Turkish siege attempt.

1805–15 Napoleon's troops twice occupy Vienna. After his defeat, the Congress of Vienna imposes order on Europe.

1848 Eighteen-year-old Franz Joseph becomes emperor.

1867 Austro-Hungarian Monarchy created.

1916 Franz Joseph dies. The Habsburg Empire is dissolved in 1918.

1922 Vienna becomes one of the Federal States of the Republic of Austria.

1934 Civil War breaks out. Clerico-Fascist dictatorship under Engelbert Dollfuss follows.

1938 Hitler annexes Austria.

1945–55 Vienna is under joint Allied control until the State Treaty restores a free Austrian state.

1995 Austria joins the European Union.

2000 The far right Freedom Party controversially joins the government coalition.

2008 A new coalition of Social Democrats and Conservatives is formed.

2013–14 Werner Faymann, head of the Social Democratic Party, is named for the second time as Austria's Federal Chancellor.

THE RINGSTRASSE

On Christmas Day 1857 Emperor Franz Joseph ordered the demolition of the city bastions and the creation of a great boulevard around the city. The Ringstrasse symbolized an era of wealth, industry and modernization.

THE *ANSCHLUSS*

After the *Anschluss*—the annexation of Austria to Germany by Adolf Hitler—many Viennese went into exile, and artistic and academic talent was lost through Austrian-born Adolf Eichmann's campaign to make Vienna *judenrein* (Jew-free).

Habsburg crown; double-headed eagle; Strauss Monument; Secession's dome of gilded laurel leaves (left to right)

Index

Vienna 25 Best

WRITTEN BY Louis James
UPDATED BY Mark Baker
SERIES EDITOR Clare Ashton
COVER DESIGN Chie Ushio, Yuko Inagaki
DESIGN WORK Tracey Freestone
IMAGE RETOUCHING AND REPRO Jacqueline Street-Elkayam

Published in the United Kingdom by AA Publishing

ISBN 978-1-1018-7950-4

SIXTH EDITION

Color separation by AA Digital Department
Printed and bound by Leo Paper Products, China

10 9 8 7 6 5 4 3 2 1

A05314
Maps in this title produced from mapping data supplied by Global Mapping, Brackley, UK © Global Mapping
Transport map © Communicarta Ltd, UK

Automobile Association would like to thank the following photographers, mpanies and picture libraries for their assistance in the preparation of this book.

18t © Österreich Werbung/Wiesenhofer; 4tl AA/J Smith; 5 AA/J Smith; 6cl © terreich Werbung/Markowitsch; 6c © Österreich Werbung/Trumler; 6cr AA/J ith; 6bl © Österreich Werbung/Bartl; 6bc AA/Clive Sawyer; 6br David Noble; © Österreich Werbung/Bartl; 7c AA/J Smith; 7cr © Österreich Werbung/Bartl; AA/J Smith; 7bc AA/Terry Harris; 7br © Österreich Werbung/Bartl; 10/11tc © terreich Werbung/Bartl; 10c © Österreich Werbung/Bartl; 10/11bc AA/J Smith; 0/11b © Österreich Werbung/Kalmar; 11c © Österreich Werbung/Bartl; 13tl AA/ avid Noble; 13c B.O'Kane/Alamy; 13b © Österreich Werbung/Kalmar; 14tr AA/J ith; 14tcr AA/J Smith; 14cbr AA/J Smith; 14br AA/David Noble; 15b AA/J Smith; © Österreich Werbung/Trumler; 16tcr © Österreich Werbung/Kalmar; 16bcr M Siebert; 16br Szaszi Hüte; 17tl AA/J Smith; 17tcl © Österreich Werbung/ mar; 17bcl © Österreich Werbung/Bartl; 17bl © Österreich Werbung/Popp 18tr AA/J Smith; 18tcr © Österreich Werbung/Markowitsch; 18bcr AA/Clive wyer; 18br Stockbyte Royalty Free; 19(i) © Österreich Werbung/Lammerhuber; (ii) AA; 19(iii) AA/J Smith; 19(iv) AA/J Smith; 19(v) AA/J Smith; 20/21 AA/J nith; 24tl F1online digitale Bildagentur GmbH/Alamy; 24tr imageBROKER/ amy; 25tl © Österreich Werbung/Diejun; 25tc AA/J Smith; 25tr AA/J Smith; 26l Clive Sawyer; 26tr AA/Clive Sawyer; 26/27c AA/J Smith; 27t AA/J Smith; 27cr /J Smith; 28tl AA/J Smith; 28tr AA/J Smith; 29tl © Österreich Werbung/Muhr; tr © Österreich Werbung/Muhr; 30tl © Österreich Werbung/Trumler ; 30tc © terreich Werbung/Trumler; 30tr © Österreich Werbung/Trumler; 31tl AA/J Smith; r AA/J Smith; 32–35t AA/J Smith; 32bl AA/J Smith; 33bl AA/J Smith; 33br AA/J ith; 34bl AA/David Noble; 34br AA/J Smith; 35b AA/J Smith; 36t AA/J Smith; 37 A/J Smith; 38–40t © Österreich Werbung/H. Wiesenhofer; 41–42t © Österreich Werbung/Wiesenhofer; 43–45t AA/Clive Sawyer; 46 © Österreich Werbung/Bartl; 7 © Österreich Werbung/Haase; 50tl © Österreich Werbung/Kalmar; 50tc AA/J Smith; 50tr AA/J Smith; 51tl AA/J Smith; 51tr AA/J Smith; 52l AA/J Smith; 52tr © Österreich Werbung/Trumler; 52/53c © Österreich Werbung/H. Wiesenhofer; 53t © Österreich Werbung/Bohnacker; 53c © Österreich Werbung/Kalmar; 54tl AA/J Smith; 54tr © Österreich Werbung/ Bartl; 55tl AA/David Noble; 55tr AA/J Smith; 56tl AA/J Smith; 56tr AA/J Smith; 57–58t AA/J Smith; 57bl AA/J Smith; 57br AA/J Smith; 58bl AA/J Smith; 58br AA/J Smith; 59t AA/J Smith; 60t © Österreich Werbung/H. Wiesenhofer; 61t © Österreich Werbung/Wiesenhofer; 62–63t AA/ Clive Sawyer; 64 AA/J Smith; 65 AA/J Smith; 68l AA/J Smith; 68/69 AA/J Smith; 69t © Österreich Werbung/Kalmar; 69b Gaia Vittoria Marturano/Alamy; 70tl AA/J mith; 70tr © Österreich Werbung/Diejun; 71t A/J Smith; 71bl AA/M Siebert; 72t A/J Smith; 73t © Österreich Werbung/H. Wiesenhofer; 74t © Österreich Werbung/ iesenhofer; 75t AA/Clive Sawyer; 76 Simon Reddy/Alamy; 77 AA/J Smith; 80tl A/J Smith; 80tr AA/J Smith; 81tl AA/Michael Siebert; 81tc AA/J Smith; 81tr AA/J ith; 82l AA/J Smith; 82tr AA/J Smith; 82/83c AA/J Smith; 83t AA/J Smith; c AA/J Smith; 84tl AA/J Smith; 84tr AA/J Smith; 85t AA/J Smith; 85b F1online ale Bildagentur GmbH/Alamy; 86t AA/J Smith; 87t © Österreich Werbung/H. iesenhofer; 88t © Österreich Werbung/Wiesenhofer; 89t AA/Clive Sawyer; 90 uboImages srl/Alamy; 91 © Österreich Werbung/Hedgecoe (London); 94tl John Peter Photography/Alamy; 94tr Viennaslide/Alamy; 95tl © Österreich Werbung/H. Wiesenhofer; 95tr © Österreich Werbung/Wiesenhofer; 96tl AA/J Smith; 96tr © Österreich Werbung/Diejun; 97 Grethe Ulgjell/Alamy; 98tl AA/J Smith; 98tr Michael Siebert; 99tl AA/J Smith; 99tr © Österreich Werbung/Bartl; 100b AA/J Smith; 101b © Österreich Werbung/Wiesenhofer; 102–104t © Österreich Werbung/Diejun; 105t © Österreich Werbung/H. Wiesenhofer; 105c © Österreich Werbung/Wiesenhofer; 106t AA/Clive Sawyer; 107 AA/J Smith; 108–112t AA/Clive Sawyer; 108tr AA/J Smith; 108tcr dpa picture alliance/Alamy; 108cr © Österreich Werbung/Kalmar; 108br © Österreich Werbung/Kalmar; 113 AA; 114–125t AA/J Smith; 122cr AA/J Smith; 122br AA/J Smith; 124bl © Österreich Werbung/Wiesenhofer; 124br © Österreich Werbung/Wiesenhofer; 125bl AA/J Smith; 125br AA/J Smith.

Every effort has been made to trace the copyright holders, and we apologize in advance for any unintentional omissions or errors. We would be pleased to apply any corrections in a following edition of this publication.

Titles in the Series

- Amsterdam
- Bangkok
- Barcelona
- Boston
- Brussels and Bruges
- Budapest
- Chicago
- Dubai
- Dublin
- Edinburgh
- Florence
- Hong Kong
- Istanbul
- Krakow
- Las Vegas
- Lisbon
- London
- Madrid
- Melbourne
- Milan
- Montréal
- Munich
- New York City
- Orlando
- Paris
- Rome
- San Francisco
- Seattle
- Shanghai
- Singapore
- Sydney
- Tokyo
- Toronto
- Venice
- Vienna
- Washington, D.C.